W9-CHV-364

School Desegregation Policy

Lexington Books Politics of Education Series
Frederick M. Wirt, Editor

Michael W. Kirst, Ed., *State, School, and Politics: Research Directions*

Joel S. Berke, Michael W. Kirst, *Federal Aid to Education: Who Benefits? Who Governs?*

Al J. Smith, Anthony Downs, M. Leanne Lachman, *Achieving Effective Desegregation*

Kern Alexander, K. Forbis Jordan, *Constitutional Reform of School Finance*

George R. LaNoue, Bruce L. R. Smith, *The Politics of School Decentralization*

David J. Kirby, T. Robert Harris, Robert L. Crain, Christine H. Rossell, *Political Strategies in Northern School Desegregation*

Philip K. Piele, John Stuart Hall, *Budgets, Bonds, and Ballots: Voting Behavior in School Financial Elections*

John C. Hogan, *The Schools, the Courts, and the Public Interest*

Jerome T. Murphy, *State Education Agencies and Discretionary Funds: Grease The Squeaky Wheel*

Howard Hamilton, Sylvan Cohen, *Policy-Making by Plebiscite: School Referenda*

Daniel J. Sullivan, *Public Aid to Nonpublic Schools*

James Hottois, Neal A. Milner, *The Sex Education Controversy: A Study of Politics, Education, and Morality*

Lauriston R. King, *The Washington Lobbyists for Higher Education*

Frederick M. Wirt, Ed., *The Polity of the School: New Research in Educational Politics*

Peter J. Cistone, Ed., *Understanding School Boards: Problems and Prospects*

Lawrence E. Gladieux, Thomas R. Wolanin, *Congress and the Colleges: The National Politics of Higher Education*

Dale Mann, *The Politics of Administrative Representation: School Administrators and Local Democracy*

Harrell R. Rodgers, Jr., Charles S. Bullock III, *Coercion to Compliance*

Richard A. Dershimer, *The Federal Government and Educational R&D*

Tyll van Geel, *Authority to Control the School Program*

Andrew Fishel, Janice Pottker, *National Politics and Sex Discrimination in Education*

Chester E. Finn, Jr., *Education and the Presidency*

Frank W. Lutz, Laurence Iannoccone, *Public Participation in Local School Districts*

Paul Goldstein, *Changing the American Schoolbook*

Everett F. Cataldo, Micheal W. Giles, Douglas S. Gatlin, *School Desegregation Policy: Compliance, Avoidance, and the Metropolitan Remedy*

School Desegregation Policy

Compliance, Avoidance, and the Metropolitan Remedy

Everett F. Cataldo
The Cleveland State University

Micheal W. Giles
Florida Atlantic University

Douglas S. Gatlin
Florida Atlantic University

Lexington Books
D. C. Heath and Company
Lexington, Massachusetts
Toronto

Library of Congress Cataloging in Publication Data

Cataldo, Everett F.
School desegregation policy.

Includes index.
1. School integration—United States.
I. Giles, Micheal W., joint author. II. Gatlin, Douglas S., joint author. III. Title.
LC214.2.C38 370.19'342 77-6080
ISBN 0-669-01536-9

 This book was prepared with the support of NSF Grant GI-34955. However, any opinions, findings, conclusions or recommendations herein are those of the authors and do not necessarily reflect the view of the NSF.

Published simultaneously in Canada

Printed in the United States of America

International Standard Book Number: 0-669-01536-9

Library of Congress Catalog Card Number: 77-6080

To three distinguished teachers and scholars

LJRH
HWK
DRM

with admiration and gratitude

Contents

List of Tables ix

Preface xi

Introduction xiii

Chapter 1 Understanding the Problem of Avoidance

Forms of Avoidance 1
Avoidance and Resegregation 2
Ramifications of Avoidance 4
Research on Avoidance 5
Avoidance Clarified 9

Chapter 2 Setting of the Study

Background 15
The Study Districts 16
Dynamics of Desegregation 20
The Private School Movement 24

Chapter 3 Data and Methods

Sampling Procedures 31
Sample Description 32
Sources of Data 33
Fieldwork 33

Chapter 4 The Avoiders: Who Are They?

Social Status and Avoidance 35
Religious Affiliation 37
Regional Origin 37
Attitudes and Avoidance 38
Commitment to the Public Schools 45
Profiles of Avoidance 48
Racism, Avoidance, and Protest: A Final Word 50

Chapter 5 The Costs of Compliance

Busing 54
School Characteristics 57

School Quality 63
The Potential of Avoidance 67
The Policymaker's Costs 68

Chapter 6 **Black and White Parental Support for School Desegregation: Some Similarities and Differences**

Parental Views of Desegregation in Practice 72
Attitudes toward Desegregation in Principle 73
Attitudes toward the Legitimacy of Government Action 75
The Impacts of Desegregation Plan Features 77
The Influence of Perceived Educational Quality and Discipline 84
The Process of Desegregation Policymaking and Parental Support 86
Putting It All Together: The Determinants of Parental Support 91

Chapter 7 **Desegregation and Educational Planning** 99

Index 103

About the Authors 111

List of Tables

2–1 School District Characteristics, 1972 20

2–2 Racial Balances in Schools, 1968–72 22

2–3 Busing Rates Before and After Implementation of Desegregation 23

2–4 Comparison of Private and Public School Enrollment Growth, K–12, 1970–73 25

2–5 Private School Enrollments, by Type, 1970–73 26

3–1 School Attendance Figures in Seven Counties, 1972–73 32

4–1 Social Status and Avoidance 36

4–2 Attitudes and Avoidance 40

4–3 Trust and Avoidance 45

4–4 Participation and Avoidance 47

5–1 Means of Getting to School 55

5–2 Distance to School 56

5–3 Percent Black School Enrollments 58

5–4 Previous Status of the Public School 59

5–5 Racial Mix of Area 61

6–1 "In General, How Do You Feel About the Way Desegregation Has Been Handled around Here?" 73

6–2 Basic Attitudes Concerning School Desegregation 74

6–3 Percent Black Enrollment and Percent Approving of Local Desegregation 77

6–4 Change in Percent Black Enrollment (1971–72 to 1972–73) and Percent Approving of Local Desegregation 78

6–5 Distance and Percent Approving of the Handling of Desegregation 81

6–6 Mean Support for Local Handling of Desegregation among White Integrationists and Segregationists, According to Plan Feature Impacts 83

6–7 Perceptions of School Quality and Discipline by Race 85

6–8 Support for the Handling of Desegregation: Multiple Correlation and Regression Analysis 93

Preface

The study reported in this book grew from a modest idea into a large-scale research project conducted at Florida Atlantic University from 1972–75 under generous support from the National Science Foundation, Division of Advanced Productivity Research and Technology.

From the time we started to the present we have become indebted to many people. To our research assistants, Emilie Rappoport, Julie Shih, and Deborah Athos for their tireless and considerable contributions. To school administrators throughout Florida without whose cooperation and support the project would have floundered. To Robert Crain, Edgar Epps, Joe Feagin, Carolyn Glieter, Ples Griffin, Mark Lohman, Gary Orfield, Ray Rist, Charles U. Smith, and Meyer Weinberg, who made many helpful suggestions during various stages of the study. To William Lucas, Trudi Miller Lucas, and James Cowhig for their substantive contributions and patient guidance in carrying the study out and bringing it to conclusion. To Fred Wirt for his invaluable help in converting a technical report into a readable manuscript. To Leslie Bowman, Katie Hanrahan, and Diane Burgess for typing various drafts and the final version of the manuscript. In expressing our deepest gratitude for the help of all these people and for what we learned from them, we also take full responsibility for what we failed to learn and for the errors of omission or commission that may appear in this book.

Each of the coauthors assumed primary responsibility for different parts of the book. Giles drafted Chapters 4 and 5; Gatlin drafted Chapter 6; and Cataldo drafted the Introduction, Chapters 1, 2, 3 and 7, and also edited the manuscript. This division of labor, however, tells an incomplete story of authorship. We have labored as close colleagues for several years, sharing the workload, exchanging ideas, and attempting, over the long run, to impose a unified focus on our work representing an amalgamation of our various thoughts. Inevitably, then, there is something of each coauthor in all the chapters of this book, and we jointly share the responsibility for what appears in these pages.

Introduction

Years after the Supreme Court's famous *Brown* v. *Board of Education* decisions, school desegregation remains a contentious and volatile issue. Federal court decisions continue to be enmeshed in controversy; calm communities often split sharply on the issue; and violent responses to desegregation orders in some northern cities in the 1970s have evoked memories of southern reactions in the 1950s.

To some observers, school desegregation appears to defy a stable, lasting solution. The apparent agelessness of the issue is explained partly by the laborious, time-consuming policymaking system of American government. Multiple decision-making points exist across different branches of government at the national, state, and local levels. Even at its most efficient, the system operates with considerable discontinuity and fragmentation, precluding quick or conclusive policy outcomes.

Thus, school desegregation policy was initiated through the U.S. Supreme Court in 1954 and 1955, then spread to lower federal courts. Ten years passed before the President and Congress fully joined the school desegregation policy process with enactment of the Civil Rights Act of 1964 and the Elementary and Secondary Education Act of 1965. Several more years passed before pressure from the federal level produced meaningful desegregation at the state and local levels across the South. Scarcely had desegregation been implemented in the South when the process began anew as school districts elsewhere in the country became targets of desegregation suits.

But it is not the process alone that explains the continuing controversy over school desegregation. The issue itself has stirred sectional antagonisms of long standing and has challenged the nation anew to confront its problem of race relations, this time in connection with one of the nation's most important institutions, the public schools.

The willingness of Americans to tax and spend heavily for education has reflected a remarkable faith in the efficacy of education for individual and collective progress. Americans have believed in economic competition and the survival of the fittest in the marketplace; but the harsher aspects of social Darwinism in American life have long been tempered by a corresponding belief that all should have an equal start in the competition through a good education. The American ideology may accept economic inequalities that reflect differences in talents and motivation to succeed, but it seems to reject a rigid class system based on privilege alone.

This American attitude toward public education was best expressed in an address by President Kennedy on June 11, 1963, following George

Wallace's "stand in the schoolhouse door" at the University of Alabama:[1]

> This is one country. It has become one country because all of us and all the people who came here had an equal chance to develop their talents.
>
> . . . Therefore I'm asking for your help in making it easier . . . to give a chance for every child to be educated to the limit of his talent.
>
> As I've said before, not every child has an equal talent or an equal ability or equal motivation. But they should have the equal right to develop their talent and their ability and their motivation to make something of themselves. . . .

Thus, Americans have believed that the public schools provide a leveling influence, a place where background liabilities might be overcome and the promise of equality realized.

The effort to extend equal educational rights to black children, however, has met considerable resistance. In the South, the *Brown* decisions revitalized a moribund Ku Klux Klan. White Citizens Counsels were formed and black students attempting to enter white schools were confronted with organized intimidation and violence. The Supreme Court, in fact, had anticipated public hostility and recognized that change would not come immediately. *Brown II* (1955) required "good faith" efforts to dismantle dual school systems "with all deliberate speed." Limited delay was permitted if a local school board could establish its necessity in the public interest.[2] The Court, however, would not allow the issue to be governed by intimidation and violence. In *Cooper* v. *Aaron,* the court denied a requested stay of a 1958 desegregation plan by the Little Rock School Board, stating that the constitutional rights of black students would not be "sacrificed or yielded to . . . violence and disorder."[3]

While recent events in places like Boston, Louisville, and Pontiac have served as grim reminders of earlier times, violent reactions to desegregation have abated considerably. Resistance, however, is not a thing of the past. The appearance of whites at the time of desegregation used to be feared. Now what is feared the most is that whites will not appear when desegregation is scheduled to begin. The form of resistance has changed, but its implications are as serious as ever. Earlier, resistance thwarted the start of school desegregation; now it may threaten its outcome.

School desegregation involves ordinary citizens as key policy actors to a far greater extent than most public issues. The outcome of school desegregation relies on compliance with the law. For officials compliance is mandatory; for citizens it is voluntary. The facts of a particular desegregation case may result in a decision requiring the school board to desegregate. The board then has no legal choice but to respond affirmatively. Citizens, however, may respond in ways extending beyond the coercive power of the law. People who live in a desegregated district are not required to remain there or to enroll their children in the public schools, but only to send their children to some school or to provide an equivalent educational opportunity. It is difficult to think of a more important or far-reaching policy issue in which the ability of citizens has been greater to avoid the law without breaking it. Citizens may avoid desegregation through the entirely legitimate expedients of making a residential move or choosing the private school alternative.

Avoidance is a polite term for "white flight" from desegregated schools. Just how much flight occurs when the schools are desegregated is a question of considerable controversy. Why it occurs is virtually unknown. There is a good deal of guesswork as to why some parents avoid sending their children to desegregated schools. Almost everyone has an opinion, but virtually no one has any hard evidence. Some contend that flight is the result of busing, or the demise of the neighborhood school, or concerns about educational quality or school safety and discipline. Others argue that avoidance is the consequence of racial or class prejudice, weak leadership or peer pressure, fear or just plain ignorance about the schools.

The lack of knowledge about such an important phenomenon is alarming. Every day local officials somewhere in the nation are making important decisions about school desegregation without knowing just what outcomes their actions are likely to produce. Every session Congress debates the busing issue without knowing what the consequences of busing have been. Federal judges concerned about community acceptance may choose one desegregation plan over another without really knowing which plan is likely to work best. Many parents are bewildered when desegregation comes to their school districts because they have no facts against which to gauge emotional appeals.

Who avoids school desegregation? What factors influence the avoidance decision? Are those factors within or beyond the ability of school policymakers to control? These are the central questions addressed in this book.

The discussion about school desegregation and white flight has been oversimplified. School desegregation is complex. The methods for achieving it differ from district to district and even within districts. Reactions to desegregation are not uniform because people differ in their personal characteristics. It is misleading to think that school desegregation means the same thing everywhere or to think that all people are alike. School desegregation might well be accompanied by avoidance. However, it may not be an inevitable result of desegregation itself, but rather a function of the manner or ways in which desegregation is implemented in particular cases, or because of the characteristics of people in particular districts. Rather than asking whether school desegregation leads to "white flight," we should ask the question: What aspects of desegregation planning produce a tendency to avoid and among what types of people? Once this question is explored it may be possible to frame desegregation plans that satisfy constitutional requirements and, at the same time, enhance the prospects for community acceptance.

The plan of this book is as follows. Chapter 1 examines the dimensions and ramifications of avoidance. Previous research is discussed and the purpose of this study is stated in detail. Chapter 2 describes the setting of the study. Chapter 3 focuses on data and research methods. Chapter 4 provides a profile of avoiders in terms of socioeconomic status, attitudes, and involvement with the public schools. Chapter 5 examines the web of influences within which avoidance decisions are made. Chapter 6 compares and contrasts support for desegregation among black and white parents. The concluding chapter summarizes the presentation and discusses its policy implications.

Notes

1. Anthony Lewis and the New York Times, *Portrait of a Decade* (New York: Random House, 1964), p. 195.
2. *Brown* v. *Board of Education—II,* 349 U.S. 294 (1955).
3. *Cooper* v. *Aaron,* 358 U.S. 1 (1958).

1 Understanding the Problem of Avoidance

The primary goal of desegregation policy is to produce an equitable, workable remedy for a constitutional violation. Over the years the courts have defined with reasonable clarity what constitutes a violation—racial separation of students in the public schools by law or through deliberate actions of officials operating under the authority of the law.[1] The courts have also made it clear that the primary responsibility for producing a remedy lies with those who have committed the violation.[2]

Even under the best of circumstances, school desegregation is a difficult task. The logistics of desegregation plans may be quite demanding, particularly in large school districts with long histories of segregation. In those districts considerable advance preparation, testing, and modification are often required before an acceptable plan is in place. Had the implementation effort in the South proceeded with reasonably good faith, school desegregation policy might have taken a different turn. Ten years after *Brown I* and *II*, however, schools in the deep South remained almost totally segregated.[3] State and local policymaking elites—governors, state legislators, school boards—refused to comply meaningfully with the *Brown* decisions and with subsequent lower federal court decisions, responding instead with defiance or tactics of evasion and delay.[4] The problem of formulating and testing remedies, therefore, was compounded by prolonged elite noncompliance whose resolution dominated school desegregation policy for many years.

Elite resistance in the South was finally broken, but not until the late 1960s, when, finally, mounting judicial pressure and federal legislation (the Civil Rights Act of 1964 and the Elementary and Secondary Education Act of 1965) combined to produce decisive legal, administrative, and financial sanctions against elite noncompliance.[5] State and local officials were, in a word, coerced to comply.[6] But while officials who refuse to comply with court orders to desegregate face penalties under the law, ordinary citizens may avoid desegregation without necessarily breaking the law.

Forms of Avoidance

In particular, three forms of legally permissible avoidance are available to parents with school children. The first may be called intrasystem avoidance, whereby a student attends a school in the same district other than the one originally assigned under a desegregation plan. This may be accomplished by a residential move of the family from the attendance zone of the assigned school into the atendance zone of another school, or by moving the student to the home of a relative or friend in a different attendance zone, or through approval by school authorities of a request to transfer from one school to another.

The second is intersystem avoidance, which results in a student's leaving public school in one district to enroll in public school in another district. This type of avoidance may be accomplished, again, by a family residential move, or by moving the student to the home of a relative or friend in another district.

The third form may be called extrasystem avoidance, whereby public schools are avoided altogether simply by enrolling the student in private school instead. Obviously, this type of avoidance does not necessitate a residential move or authorization from public school officials, but only a personal decision on the part of parents to abandon public school in favor of private school.

Typically, it is white parents who are most likely to avoid school desegregation. Thus, avoidance has become known, colloquially, as "white flight." As the foregoing discussion indicates, however, it is important to distinguish between different forms of "white flight." Intrasystem avoidance represents flight from a particular public school. Intersystem avoidance represents flight from a particular public school district. Extrasystem avoidance represents flight from the public schools altogether.

Avoidance and Resegregation

As any of these forms of flight occur they may contribute to resegregation of the schools. Resegregation is the tendency for the racial balance in schools affected by desegregation to shift in such a manner as to recreate a segregated educational environment. For example, a previously black elementary school may be desegregated by changing its attendance zone to include white neighborhoods, with a planned racial balance of 60 percent white/40 percent black. However, significant residential movement to other neighborhoods in the district occurs among white parents with children assigned to that school, and the school opens with an enrollment 60 percent black/40 percent white. Moreover, throughout the school year families continue to move, so that by the end of the year the school's racial balance is 80 percent black/20 percent white. That school can then be classified as largely resegregated. Corresponding to the type of avoidance occurring, this may be called intrasystem resegregation.

Or a district may plan to desegregate all of its schools so that the racial balance in each school reflects the racial balance between students in the district overall, for example, 65 percent white/35 percent black. At the opening of the year racial balances in the schools are approximately 55 percent white/45 percent black and, by the end of the second year of desegregation, 65 percent black/35 percent white, clearly showing a tendency toward resegregation in that district's schools. If the pattern of avoidance is to a nearby public school district not undergoing desegregation, the result may be classified as intersystem resegregation. If it is to private schools, then extrasystem resegregation has occurred.

The type of avoidance and, correspondingly, the form of the resegregation problem may depend on the dimensions and timing of desegregation planning and the jurisdictional characteristics of the school districts. When a desegregation plan does not affect all the schools within a district in similar fashion selective intrasystem avoidance may occur, thereby producing resegregation tendencies in some schools but not in others. For example, when the schools in Mobile, Alabama, were desegregated two high schools fell far short of their expected white enrollment, while a third high school exceeded its anticipated white enrollment by nearly 20 percent.[7] Apparently a similar situation has occurred in the Louisville area through the use of a rather permissive transfer policy established by the consolidated Louisville/Jefferson County school authorities.[8]

By contrast, when a desegregation plan has a more uniform impact on all district schools, intrasystem avoidance may not be a viable option. The conditions for which parents might want to avoid one particular school in the district may prevail to a significant degree in all the schools. Whether avoidance is of the intersystem or extrasystem variety may then depend on the jurisdictional boundaries of school districts and the timing of desegregation. In areas where school district boundaries are contiguous with municipal subdivision boundaries it may be possible for parents to avoid desegregation in one district by conveniently moving to an adjoining municipality where desegregation is not occurring. The result is intersystem resegregation.

The recent research of James S. Coleman may provide an example of this phenomenon.[9] Examining trends over time in school districts in metropolitan areas, Coleman contends that a reduction of segregation within central city school districts leads to an increase in segregation between those city school districts and outlying school districts within their metropolitan areas.[10] Simply put, Coleman claims that when central city schools desegregate, whites flee to the predominantly white suburban schools, causing central city schools to resegregate.

Intersystem avoidance is still possible, but perhaps more difficult, when school district jurisdiction encompasses the entire county. Under this condition it is not possible to avoid central city desegregation by moving to an adjacent suburb because desegregation occurs across city-suburban lines. Avoiders would have to move beyond the county line, and the greater distance and inconvenience might lead them to stay where they are but place their children in private school. The likelihood of extrasystem avoidance is enhanced further when neighboring county school districts are desegregating at approximately the same time.

This situation characterized most of the South, where county school systems predominate and where substantial desegregation began to occur simultaneously throughout the region, leaving segregated private schools the most realistic alternative to desegregating public schools. The number of private schools grew rapidly as public school desegregation spread across the South. A *New York Times* survey found that 700 all-white private schools had been established in eleven southern states from 1965–70, 300 of them in 1970 alone.[11] Private school enrollments in the South mushroomed over the same period, reaching an estimated 500,000 by the school year 1971–72.[12] Meanwhile, many southern public school districts experienced declining white enrollments. By 1967, Surrey County, Virginia, lost all of its white pupils, and by 1970, Wilkerson County, Mississippi, experienced a similar phenomenon.[13] A suit to desegregate Atlanta's public schools was brought in 1958, when the schools were 70 percent white and 30 percent black. By 1971, that ratio was reversed.[14] In 1970, the schools in Jackson, Mississippi, enrolled 40,000 students, 55 percent of whom were white. Jackson's "freedom-of-choice" plan was struck down in the middle of 1970–71 and replaced by a court-ordered desegregation plan. By 1972, white enrollment in the schools had decreased by 10,500 and the schools were 64 percent black.[15]

In the South, therefore, avoidance has been largely of the extrasystem variety, and the resegregation problem there seems best understood in terms of rejection of the public schools in favor of private schools.

Ramifications of Avoidance

The issue of "white flight" has become more prominent as the educational implications of avoidance are more widely recognized. As just seen, by contributing to resegregation, a substantial amount of avoidance could produce an outcome that desegregation was specifically intended to prevent—racial isolation in the schools.[16]

Avoidance may create serious problems in other respects as well. Avoidance arises from dissatisfaction with or opposition to school desegregation policy in some form. In American society it has been taken as axiomatic that public institutions cannot function effectively without broadly based public support. To the extent that negative reactions to desegregation may erode support for the schools, then public perceptions of the schools' educational effectiveness, trust, and confidence in school leadership and willingness to support the schools financially may decline accordingly.[17] If avoidance leads to enrollment declines, the per pupil costs of education will increase, and state funds may be lost when such support is tied by formula to average daily attendance.[18]

The apparent tendency of avoidance to stimulate private school growth poses a number of problems for public education. For a variety of reasons, qualified teachers and administrators may follow the students to private schools.[19] Professional mobility is not of itself wrong, but if the opportunity structure for such mobility feeds on public resentment of desegregation, the situation may be socially unhealthy and subversive of the goal of a decent education for all students, irrespective of race and type of school.

Avoidance may be financially costly for individuals, and perhaps only more well-to-do families can afford a residential move or the payment of public school taxes and private school tuitions at the same time. The role of public schools in American society and the value of public education could change substantially if avoidance creates a notable class-based distinction between public school enrollment and private school attendance. Irrespective of race, lower-class students, then, could be consigned to what may be viewed as second-class educational citizenship in the public schools.[20]

The educational effects of desegregation have been debated widely.[21] Some studies suggest, however, that the initial progress of black students, measured by standardized test scores, is associated significantly with the classroom presence of white students of higher class standing.[22] Avoidance could eliminate this apparent advantage, and also an important socializing experience for the white students.[23]

For reasons such as these, school desegregation policy has been seriously questioned of late, even by legal scholars.[24] Further, attempts have been made to introduce evidence of "white flight" into recent major desegregation cases, with some success. For example, in the Indianapolis case, the district court declined to order immediate desegregation, fearing an "accelerated and irreversible" exodus of white students.[25] In the Dayton case, the U.S. Department of Justice has recently warned against using the "white flight" thesis as grounds for delaying or limiting a remedy for a constitutional violation.[26]

Research on Avoidance

Scholarship on the topic of avoidance has expanded lately, providing the opportunity to inform policymaking through academic research. The studies to date, however, have a number of liabilities which limit their policy utility.

First, there is often a failure to distinguish between the sources of school desegregation: governmental action which is, by definition, official policy versus racial succession in neighborhoods which is not. Second, it seems uniformly unrecognized that there are different forms of avoidance which produce different policy outcomes. Third, the most commonly used measure of avoidance—aggregate change in percent white school enrollments—may measure other things as well, thereby producing misleading findings. Fourth, there has been virtually no detailed examination of characteristics of avoiders or specific conditions under which avoidance occurs. This makes it impossible to determine the policy factors associated with avoidance.

The problem of policy utility is perhaps best seen in studies of desegregation in schools that results simply from racial succession in neighborhoods. For example, a study by Arthur L. Stinchcombe and others concluded that once a school was desegregated the proportion of black students increased steadily each year thereafter.[27] The study, however, was conducted in Baltimore, Maryland, where school desegregation was closely associated with racial transition in the neighborhoods. Increases in percent black in the schools reflected increases in percent black in their attendance zones as black immigration to the neighborhoods was accompanied by white outmigration. How is avoidance to be characterized when racial characteristics of the neighborhoods and the schools vary concurrently? Is it from the neighborhoods or from the schools? If the former, there may be relatively little that school policymakers can or legally need to do about it. If the latter, then one policy option is for officials to devise means of keeping the schools segregated while neighborhoods are desegregating. But this is precisely what the federal courts have said is prohibited by the Fourteenth Amendment.

The recent research of James S. Coleman is also flawed by the failure to distinguish between the sources of desegregation.[28] Finding an association between percent black increases in the schools and declining white enrollments, Coleman has argued for a reconsideration of court-ordered busing on the grounds that it may produce racial isolation.[29] Several of the school districts in Coleman's study, however, were not under court-ordered desegregation.[30] In those districts percent black increases in the schools largely reflected percent black increases in the neighborhoods comprising the schools' attendance zones, hardly grounds upon which to conclude that court-ordered school desegregation produces avoidance and resegregation, or that busing should be abandoned.

When schools are desegregated through governmental action residential patterns are not necessarily disturbed. By making the source of school desegregation clear, it should be possible to assess its impact on avoidance without confusion. Reynolds Farley has examined the relationship between percent white enrollment changes and changes in school segregation scores for the largest U.S. cities from 1967–72.[31] Farley found declining white enrollments to be unassociated with desegregation in the schools. This was true of seventy-five northern districts in which school desegregation occurred mostly as a result of neighborhood change, and also of fifty southern districts in which governmental action would have been the principal source of school desegregation.[32] Farley concluded that there seemed to be no significant relationship between school desegregation and "white flight."[33] A similar conclusion has emerged from a recent study by Michael R. Fitzgerald and David R. Morgan, who examined the relationship between outmigration, measured by percent white change in the schools, and school desegregation, as well as a host of economic, political, and social variables.[34] The study included 185 U.S. cities with populations of 50,000 or above in which at least 3 percent of the city school population was black. Changes in percent white enrollments were calculated over a six-year period, 1968–74. Consistent with Farley's findings, Fitzgerald and Morgan did not find declining white enrollments to be associated with their measure of school desegregation in either northern or southern school districts.[35]

There are a number of problems in these two studies with the use of the aggregate percent white change figure as a measure of avoidance. First, the extent of intrasystem avoidance could have been overlooked. Substantial shifts in white student enrollments from some schools to others could have occurred within the study districts, producing resegregative tendencies in the schools subject to avoidance. These shifts, however, would not have been captured by the overall percent white change figure across district schools if declining white enrollments in some schools were offset by increasing white enrollments in others.

Farley, and Fitzgerald and Morgan, also could have underestimated both intersystem and extrasystem avoidance. Their aggregate measure would not indicate the extent to which whites who left for other districts or for private schools following desegregation might have been replaced by nonavoiding whites entering the public schools for the first time.

Percent white change should be suspect as an indicator of avoidance on other grounds as well. Over the years covered by the analyses of Farley and of Fitzgerald and Morgan, declining white enrollments in central city schools could have been expected on the basis of natural factors alone. As a rule, central city white populations have grown significantly older than nonwhite populations, and fertility rates tend to be higher for nonwhites than for whites.[36] Consequently, the available "pool" of school-age children in central cities would have become increasingly nonwhite even without white outmigration. In light of this secular effect, the findings of Farley and of Fitzgerald and Morgan should be viewed with caution. In effect, their dependent variable is not a pure or precise measure of avoidance.

In summary, Stinchcombe and Coleman suggest that school desegregation policy produces the problem of avoidance. Their data, however, do not support this conclusion because their studies were based on or included districts in which changes in school racial balances were not the exclusive result of official policy. Farley, and Fitzgerald and Morgan, suggest that school desegregation policy does not produce avoidance. Their studies, however, are inconclusive because they are handicapped by measurement problems that may obscure the relationship.

Christine Rossell studied ''white flight'' in eighty-six northern school districts in which desegregation occurred as a result of official action, in eleven of them by court order.[37] Rossell grouped the districts according to type and amount of desegregation: (1) court ordered; (2) high desegreagtion (reassignment of more than 20 percent of the students); (3) medium desegregation (reassignment of 5 to 20 percent); (4) low desegregation (reassignment of less than 5 percent). Comparisons were made of rates of white withdrawal from the schools before and after desegregation. Overall, there was no significant increase in the rates of white withdrawal in any of the groups.[38] In the eleven court-ordered districts, only two experienced a significant increase in avoidance—Pasadena, California, and Pontiac, Michigan. They were also the only districts to show a significant increase in the rate of white withdrawal among the ten districts with the highest degree of school desegregation. Within the other groups, the number of districts experiencing a significant increase of avoidance was negligible.[39] In districts where avoidance occurred, stability was achieved by the third year following implementation of desegregation.[40] Rossell concluded that ''school desegregation has little or no effect on white flight.''[41]

By contrast, Charles Clotfelter found a significant association between school desegregation and avoidance in seventy-eight counties in Mississippi.[42] Focusing on extrasystem avoidance, Clotfelter found that public school desegregation was an important factor in the growth of private school enrollments after full-scale desegregation was implemented across Mississippi in January 1970.[43]

What accounts for the differences between the findings of Rossell and Clotfelter? Neither study confused the sources of desegregation, nor were there serious measurement problems. Was it that Rossell's study districts were in the North, whereas Clotfelter's were in the South? That all of Clotfelter's districts were under court order whereas only a small percentage of Rossell's were? Were there wide variations between social characteristics of people in the seventy-eight Mississippi districts as opposed to those in the eighty-six nonsouthern districts? Were there differences in the methods whereby desegregation was implemented?

Rossell did not examine any factors associated with avoidance. Finding that avoidance occurred typically before the opening of school in the first year of desegregation, she attributed it to ''fear of problems'' associated with desegregation.[44] Clotfelter found that private school enrollments varied directly with percent black in the school system and income.[45]

Apparently avoidance must be understood in terms of the dynamics of the desegregation process itself, and the socioeconomic characteristics of those who are affected by desegregation planning. Is fear the determining factor? Does fear vary with income or with percent black enrollment? To answer these and related questions, avoidance must be examined at the individual level, among the parents who are confronted with the decision to avoid or to comply with school desegregation.

Avoidance Clarified

To posit that desegregation produces avoidance is to say, in effect, that certain features or costs associated with school desegregation create a tendency among some parents to avoid a particular school, an entire school district, or the public schools altogether. Faced with a decree to desegregate, school authorities implement the policy by developing desegregation plans. These plans, however, vary from district to district, and the effects of desegregation plan features even vary within the same district. Some school children are scheduled to ride a bus; others are not. Busing distances are longer for some children than for others. Some children may be sent to schools with majority black enrollments, others to predominantly white schools. Within the latter category, the proportion nonwhite could range from below 10 percent to nearly 50 percent. Some children may continue to attend schools within their neighborhoods; others may be transferred to other schools outside their neighborhoods. Some may be transferred for most of their school years, others for only a few. There is, therefore, no uniform desegregation stimulus to which individuals respond, but rather a variety of stimuli imposing different costs on different individuals.

Since desegregation plans vary in their costs, they may also vary in their outcomes. Avoidance, therefore, may depend not simply on whether desegregation occurs, but on how it occurs. Avoidance may be more likely among parents whose children face the costs of busing, reassignment far away from their neighborhoods or for most of their school years, or assignment to schools with higher black ratios. Avoidance may be less likely among parents whose children do not face those costs.

As desegregation plans differ in their costs, so also do the individuals upon whom the costs are assessed. Since avoidance is a personal decision, an individual act, its incidence may be conditioned by the socio-attitudinal characteristics of those affected. Racial and class stereotypes or prejudices, attitudes toward desegregation or those responsible for it, social status, cultural upbringing, and environmental influences may affect individual perceptions of both the costs and benefits associated with school desegregation.

Avoidance imposes costs as well. A residential move could be inconvenient or financially costly or disruptive of established family patterns. The private school alternative certainly involves added financial costs. Some might view these costs as worthwhile; others might not. Some can afford them; others cannot. Avoidance, therefore, involves a readiness to act followed by the capability to act. Readiness is activated, however, by the manner in which desegregation is implemented, that is, by the costs imposed by the plan itself.

School policymakers, as we have seen, are compelled to comply with desegregation orders. They cannot in turn compel citizens to comply. However, they may be able to minimize the effects of avoidance by minimizing the costs of desegregation. Of course, officials under order to desegregate must operate within certain constraints established by the courts and by the characteristics of their school district. Courts will insist that the plan provides a workable, equitable remedy. Within the district there are certain fixed parameters within which a plan must operate: size; distribution and racial mix of the school age population; the capacity, location, and condition of school buildings; and the limits of human and financial resources. Nevertheless, a considerable degree of flexibility exists for school officials in developing and implementing a plan. The proportion black in any given school might be kept low by equalizing the black enrollment across all district schools; but it might require a good deal of busing. The incidence or distance of bus transportation might be reduced by redrawing school attendance zones, realigning grade structures, or pairing schools; but that might result in a high proportion of white students attending formerly black schools. White attendance at previously black schools might be encouraged by establishing special educational programs, rehabilitating buildings, or increasing security in and around the schools. Alternately, formerly black schools may be converted to other uses as new schools are built within relatively easy reach of both whites and blacks.

These are among the options that might be available to desegregation planners. Which ones should they choose? In each instance, the less costly one, of course. But which alternative is less costly? Low percent black or less busing? More busing or the assignment of more white students to previously black schools? Full utilization of classroom capacity or the gradual phasing out of formerly black schools? These questions cannot be answered without knowledge of how parents assess the costs of different plan options, how those assessments are conditioned by personal and environmental characteristics, and how these combined factors influence avoidance decisions.

Avoidance is a complex phenomenon. Its extent is debated intensely; its antecedents are virtually unknown. By approaching the topic from the individual level of analysis, at the parental level where the avoidance decision is made, it is hoped that a linkage can be provided between desegregation policymaking, on the one hand, and proximate policy outcomes and long-term consequences, on the other.

Notes

1. *Swann* v. *Charlotte–Mecklenburg,* 402 U.S. 1, 15 (1971).
2. Ibid.
3. U.S. Commission on Civil Rights, *Twenty Years After Brown: Equality of Educational Opportunity* (Washington, D.C., 1975), p. 50.
4. Ibid., pp. 5–10; Frank T. Read, "Judicial Evolution of the Law of School Integration Since Brown v. Board of Education," *Law and Contemporary Problems,* 39 (Winter 1975), 10–16.
5. U.S. Commission on Civil Rights, *Twenty Years After Brown,* pp. 10–23; Frank T. Read, "Law of School Integration Since Brown," 17–32. See also Gary Orfield, *The Reconstruction of Southern Education: The Schools and the 1964 Civil Rights Act* (New York: John Wiley and Sons, Inc., 1969).
6. Charles S. Bullock III, and Harrell R. Rodgers, Jr., "Coercion to Compliance: Southern School Districts and School Desegregation Guidelines," *Journal of Politics* (November 1976), 1000–1001.
7. Robert E. Anderson, "Mobile, Alabama: The Essence of Survival," in *The South and Her Children: School Desegregation, 1970–71* (Atlanta, Ga: Southern Regional Council, 1971), pp. 38–50.
8. Robert M. Williams, "What Louisville Has Taught Us About Busing," *Saturday Review,* April 30, 1977, p. 51.
9. James S. Coleman, "Liberty and Equality in School Desegregation," *Social Policy,* 6 (January/February 1976), 9–13. See also James S. Coleman, Sara D. Kelly, and John A. Moore, *Trends in School Segregation, 1968–73* (Washington, D.C.: The Urban Institute, 1975).
10. Coleman, "Liberty and Equality," 12.

11. *New York Times,* 29 August 1971, p. 37, Col. 1.

12. *New York Times,* 2 September 1972, p. 13, Col. 5.

13. Jim Leeson, "Private Schools for Whites Face Some Hurdles," *Southern Education Report,* 3 (November 1967), 13; Jerry De Muth, "Public School Turnovers in the South," *America,* November 7, 1970, p. 379.

14. John Bechler, "Has School Integration in the South Gone as Far as It Can Go?" *School Management,* 15 (October 1971), 2.

15. John Egerton, "Report Card on Southern School Desegregation," *Saturday Review,* 55 (April 1, 1972), p. 42.

16. The essence of Coleman's argument is that it has. See *Trends in School Segregation,* pp. 21–22.

17. Micheal W. Giles, Douglas S. Gatlin, and Everett F. Cataldo, "Parental Support for School Referenda," *Journal of Politics,* 38 (May 1976), 442–51.

18. Leeson, "Private Schools. . . ."

19. Ibid.

20. See Charles S. Benson, "The Transition to a New School Finance System," in John Pincus, ed., *School Finance in Transition* (Cambridge, Mass.: Ballinger Publishing Co., 1974), p. 157.

21. In a comprehensive review of the literature on the topic, see Nancy H. St. John, *School Desegregation: Outcomes for Children* (New York: John Wiley and Sons, 1975); Meyer Weinberg, "The Relationship between School Desegregation and Academic Achievement: A Review of the Research," *Law and Contemporary Problems,* 39 (Spring 1975), 241–70.

22. Robert P. O'Reilly, *Racial and Social Class Isolation in the Schools* (New York: Praeger Publishers, Inc., 1970).

23. U.S. Commission on Civil Rights, *Twenty Years After Brown,* p. 87.

24. Lino A. Graglia, *Disaster By Decree: The Supreme Court Decisions on Race and the Schools* (Ithaca, N.Y.: Cornell University Press, 1976).

25. *U.S.* v. *Board of School Commissioners, Indianapolis, Indiana* (322 F. Supp. 655) p. 676.

26. *Brinkman* v. *Gilligan,* 97 S. Ct. 2766 (1977).

27. Arthur L. Stinchcombe, Mary McDill, and Dollie Walker, "Is There a Racial Tipping Point in Changing Schools?" *Journal of Social Issues*, 25 (1969), 127–36.

28. Coleman, "Liberty and Equality"; Coleman, *Trends in School Segregation.*

29. A comprehensive critique of Coleman's position is offered by Thomas F. Pettigrew and Robert L. Green, "School Desegregation in

Large Cities: A Critique of the Coleman 'White Flight' Thesis,'' *Harvard Educational Review,* 46 (February 1976), 1–53. See also Christine Rossell, ''School Desegregation and White Flight,'' *Political Science Quarterly,* 90 (Winter 1975–76), 686–88.

30. Pettigrew and Green, ''School Desegregation in Large Cities,'' 12.

31. Reynolds Farley, ''Is Coleman Right?'' *Social Policy,* 6 (January/February 1976), 14–23.

32. Ibid., pp. 16–17.

33. Ibid., p. 17.

34. Michael R. Fitzgerald and David R. Morgan, ''Assessing the Consequences of Public Policy: School Desegregation and White Flight in Urban America.'' Paper delivered at the Annual Meeting of the Midwest Political Science Association, Chicago, Illinois, April 1977.

35. Ibid., p. 19.

36. Bureau of Census, *Statistical Abstract of the United States: 1975* (Washington, D.C.: U.S. Government Printing Office, 1975), pp. 26–27.

37. ''School Desegregation and White Flight,'' 675–95.

38. Ibid., p. 676.

39. Ibid., pp. 682–83.

40. Ibid., p. 688.

41. Ibid., p. 676.

42. Charles Clotfelter, ''School Desegregation, 'Tipping,' and Private School Enrollment,'' *Journal of Human Resources,* 11 (Winter 1976), 28–49.

43. Ibid., p. 29.

44. Rossell, ''School Desegregation and White Flight,'' 683.

45. Clotfelter, ''School Desegregation, 'Tipping,' . . . ,'' 42–47.

2 Setting of the Study

This study was conducted in seven school districts in the state of Florida. As seen in the last chapter, the configuration of school districts and the timing of desegregation have an important bearing on the options that are available for avoidance. Where school districts are area-wide, and when desegregation occurs concurrently among neighboring districts, private school is the most realistic alternative to public school. Florida's county-wide school districts were desegregated at approximately the same time. For the most part, desegregation could not be avoided by a city-to-suburb residential move or by county-to-county movement. Therefore, this study focuses on extrasystem avoidance—the rejection of public schools in favor of private academies. The data for this study cover the years in which almost all of the substantial desegregation activity occurred in Florida, 1968–74.

Background

Florida contains sixty-seven counties, each with its own independent public elementary and secondary school system.[1] Each district has an elected school board and a superintendent either elected or appointed by the board.[2] There are no separate municipal school districts within any of the counties.

Florida's county school system reflects a long-standing southern pattern of according considerable importance to county government.[3] Counties have always been important units of government in rural areas, and throughout most of its history the South was one of the most rural regions in the country. Despite rapid population growth and metropolitanization, Florida has retained county school systems. In doing so, it has kept a pattern of school administration toward which the rest of the nation has been moving in the post–World War II years. From 1949–50 to 1969–70 the number of public school districts in the United States was consolidated from over 80,000 to fewer than 20,000.[4]

Before *Brown,* Florida operated separate public schools for whites and blacks. The Florida Constitution of 1885 mandated that "white and colored children shall not be taught in the same school, but impartial provision shall be made for both."[5] Under statutory law, Florida prohibited teaching blacks and whites in the same building or class in any public or private school. School boards were required to establish separate school attendance zones for white and black students, even if they lived in the same neighborhood. School superintendents were required to keep separate books for the white and black schools.[6] Until 1954, therefore, Florida operated a classic dual school system under constitutional and statutory law.

After *Brown,* Florida passed a pupil assignment law, and "freedom of choice" plans were adopted to give the appearance of legal compliance. As elsewhere desegregation proceeded at a snail's pace. Reactions to desegregation in Florida, however, were less extreme than in many other southern states. Pressure to close the public schools in defiance was resisted. Florida was one of only three southern states not to authorize tuition grants for private nonsectarian schooling.[7]

Leroy Collins, governor from 1954–60, was widely acknowledged as a "moderate" on the desegregation issue. In 1954, Collins defeated an arch-segregationist opponent to fill an unexpired gubernatorial term. In the campaign, he pledged to preserve segregation. After reelection to a full four-year term in 1956, however, Collins began to support the *Brown* decisions and, in fact, discretely promoted some desegregation, particularly among the state's largest school systems.[8] By 1964, sixteen of Florida's sixty-seven county school districts had some desegregation; but it was merely token. Only 1.5 percent of all the state's black students were actually attending school with white students.[9]

Pressure for meaningful desegregation was kept on Florida's school districts throughout the 1960s by suits filed in federal courts and through the activities of the U.S. Departments of Justice and of Health, Education and Welfare.[10] Toward the end of the decade, some signs of real progress were apparent; and by 1972, under continued legal and administrative pressure, substantial desegregation activity was occurring throughout Florida's sixty-seven school districts.[11]

The Study Districts

The seven districts selected for this study were Dade and Palm Beach Counties, on Florida's southeastern Atlantic "Gold Coast"; Duval County, northeast on the Atlantic coast; Leon County, in north central Florida; Escambia County, in the western "panhandle"; Manatee and Lee Counties, southwest on the Gulf coast.

Dade County

Dade contains twenty-seven incorporated municipalities, including the city of Miami and a large unincorporated area.[12] According to the 1970 census, the county population was 1,267,972, the largest of Florida's Standard Metropolitan Statistical Areas.[13]

At the time of this study, the Dade County school system was the largest in Florida, and the sixth largest nationally.[14] In the school year 1972–73, Dade County's public schools enrolled 261,011 students, 26 percent of whom were black.[15]

A suit to desegregate Dade's schools was first brought in 1956. The county's first desegregation effort came in the spring of 1959 with an announcement by the school board that black students would be admitted to Orchard Villa Elementary School starting in the 1959–60 school year. Orchard Villa's attendance area consisted of neighborhoods undergoing racial transition from white to black. While blacks could start to attend the school, whites who chose not to attend could obtain a transfer to another elementary school. Two years later, Orchard Villa was a nearly all-black school.[16] As token voluntary desegregation proceeded in other schools in Dade, the county school board officially declared the system to be desegregated in June 1963.[17] The board's declaration, however, belied the fact that it was still operating an essentially dual school system. In 1968, five years after the declaration was made, 80 percent of Dade County's black students still attended schools that were 80–100 percent black in their enrollment.[18] Court pressure was kept on Dade County until the board finally mandated a district-wide desegregation plan for fall 1970. The plan was based essentially on the techniques of pairing or clustering schools coupled with busing students away from their neighborhoods when necessary. Under pairing two schools at the same grade level are coupled together, and all the students attend one school for some grades and the other school for other grades. For example, a pairing may include two elementary schools, grades K–6, one formerly black, the other formerly white. All students in the attendance zones of the two schools attend the formerly white school for grades K–3, and then move to the formerly black school for grades 4–6, thus desegregating two previously segregated elementaries. Depending on distances, some of the blacks may have to be bused for grades K–3, and some of the whites for grades 4–6. Clustering is similar to pairing, except that it involves more than two schools.[19]

Duval County

With a consolidated city/county government, Duval County (population 528,865 in 1970) is part of the large Jacksonville SMSA which includes four other small counties. With a 1972 student population of 121,855, 33 percent of them black, the Duval County school system was the third largest in the state and the twentieth largest in the nation.[20]

A suit to desegregate the Duval County schools was initiated in 1960.[21] At the time the county maintained 113 totally segregated schools, 89 of them for whites and 24 for blacks. A grade-a-year desegregation plan coupled with "freedom-of-choice" resulted in no real desegregation. By 1965 only sixty black students (out of 30,000) were attending school with whites and no white student attended a black school.[22] By 1968, over 87 percent of the black students still attended schools that were 80–100 percent black.[23] Under court order, a major desegregation plan was implemented in 1972–73. Its central feature involved clustering elementary and junior high schools located in the white preconsolidation suburbs and in black neighborhoods in the preconsolidation central city of Jacksonville. Black elementaries were converted to sixth-grade centers. Black students were then bused to formerly white elementaries for grades 1–5. In turn, white students were bused to the formerly black elementaries for the sixth grade. A similar plan was adopted for the junior highs. Formerly black junior high schools were converted to seventh-grade centers, with formerly white schools serving the eighth and ninth grades. The school board also rezoned the attendance areas of two high schools to accommodate both white and black neighborhoods and modified the patterns feeding students from junior highs to high schools.[24] A substantial amount of busing was necessary to operate the plan.[25]

Palm Beach County

A relatively large SMSA with a 1970 population of 348,993, Palm Beach County contains thirty-seven incorporated municipalities.[26] In 1972, Palm Beach County was the seventh-largest school district in Florida and ranked forty-ninth in size nationally with 75,222 students, 29 percent of whom were black.[27]

A suit to desegregate the schools was initiated shortly after *Brown II*. Over the years, the county school board allowed a very modest degree of desegregation through grade-a-year plans, freedom-of-choice, and the redrawing of some attendance zones. Still, in 1968, nearly 80 percent of the black students went to schools that were 80–100 percent black.[28]

Under court order a major desegregation plan was implemented in the fall of 1971. The plan relied mainly on target-area busing. Selected white and black neighborhoods were targeted to exchange students between schools in the residential areas, with whites being bused to the formerly black schools and blacks to the formerly white schools. In addition, junior high schools were converted to middle schools (grades 6–8), formerly black high schools were also converted to middle schools, and elementaries were restructured from K–6 to K–5.[29]

Escambia County

Located on the far western end of the Florida panhandle, Escambia County is part of the Pensacola SMSA. The 1970 population figure for Escambia was 205,334.[30] It contains only two incorporated municipalities (including Pensacola), and 71 percent of the 1970 population resided in unincorporated areas.[31] In 1972 the school district ranked tenth in size in Florida and eighty-second nationally with 51,829 students, 28 percent of whom were black.[32]

Brought to court in the early 1960s, the school board finally implemented a plan under court order in 1969. The plan relied on the techniques of pairing, converting some formerly black elementary and secondary schools to middle schools, altering the attendance zones of two high schools, and closing three black elementary schools. Busing was employed as an integral part of the plan. Transportation was provided for students reassigned to an elementary school at least one mile from home, to a middle school one-and-one-half miles from home, or to a high school two miles from home.[33]

Leon County

Home of Tallahassee, the state capital, and of two state universities, Leon County was the smallest SMSA in the state, according to the 1970 census, with a population of 103,047, and only one incorporated municipality.[34] In 1972, Leon was the seventeenth-largest school district in Florida, with 22,852 students, 33 percent of whom were black.[35]

After lengthy court proceedings desegregation was implemented under court order in September 1970. The plan was based on redrawing attendance zones for all the schools in wedge-shaped patterns outward from Tallahassee to surrounding areas. The plan sought to combine students from different socioeconomic groups as well as from each race within the attendance zone of each school.[36] The number of students transported to school and busing distances actually declined with adoption of the plan.[37]

Lee County

Located on the southwest Gulf coast, Lee County is one of the fastest-growing SMSAs in Florida and the nation. It has two incorporated municipalities, Fort Meyers and Cape Coral; but 63 percent of the 1970 population of 105,216 lived in unincorporated areas.[38] The 1972 school population was 26,795, 18 percent black, making Lee the fourteenth-largest school district in the state.[39]

As with the other districts, Lee County's desegregation plan was implemented under court order after a lengthy trial. The plan, instituted in 1969, was similar to Palm Beach's in that it used target-area busing as the primary technique.[40]

Manatee County

The only nonmetropolitan area in the study, Manatee County is located on the Gulf coast, south of the Tampa–St. Petersburg SMSA. Its 1970 population was 97,115, with Bradenton as the largest of the county's six incorporated municipalities.[41] Manatee's 1972 school population was 20,331, 22 percent of them black, making it the twentieth-largest school district in the state.[42]

Manatee's court-ordered desegregation plan began in 1970. Its features included redrawn attendance zones, modified feeder patterns, and busing.[43]

Selected characteristics for the seven districts are shown in table 2–1.

Dynamics of Desegregation

In each of the counties school desegregation was a difficult task, but it was particularly demanding in the larger, more populous districts. In each district it was necessary not only to overcome the cultural legacy of segregation, but also to demonstrate to the federal courts that every reasonable effort had been taken to establish satisfactory racial balances in a large number of schools over a very sizable area. A few examples will illustrate what was involved.

Table 2–1
School District Characteristics, 1972

School District	*Square Miles*	*No. of Schools*	*No. of Students*	*% Black*	*Implementation*
Dade	2,109	237	261,011	26.4	1970
Duval	840	142	121,855	32.6	1971–72
Escambia	757	75	51,829	28.1	1969
Lee	1,005	36	26,795	18.4	1969
Leon	696	30	22,852	33.0	1970
Manatee	785	25	20,331	21.7	1970
Palm Beach	2,578	82	75,222	28.6	1971

When the Palm Beach plan took effect, the county operated eighty-two school centers spread across 2,578 square miles, an area roughly two-and-one-half times the size of the entire state of Rhode Island.[44] The reliance on target-area busing required transporting students from their own neighborhoods to schools in other municipalities, and from unincorporated areas far inland to incorporated municipalities on the coast. Bus rides of twenty-five to thirty miles round-trip were not uncommon. Bus routes were staggered so that some students stood watch for the school bus in early morning darkness while others faced a return trip home when darkness was descending again. Some schools faced the difficult task of desegregation while, at the same time, operating on double sessions to relieve overcrowding.

Lee County's busing plan had much the same effect. With an area of 1,005 square miles, desegregating the county schools meant implementing a busing plan across an area exactly the size of the state of Rhode Island. Insofar as possible, school officials sought to maintain racial balances in the schools proportionate to the racial distribution in the system as a whole of 82 percent white/18 percent black.[45] This necessitated busing over 15,000 students each year, or 57 percent of the total enrollment in the entire school system.[46] Few students could avoid being transported over considerable distances for at least some of their school years.

Duval County ranks sixty-fourth in size among the nation's metropolitan areas and is Florida's most heavily industrialized county. The preconsolidation city of Jacksonville is bounded by the St. John's River and the Seaboard Coastline Railroad. It contains a central business district, heavy industry, a large port area, and most of the county's black population. The central feature of the desegregation plan involved clustering predominantly black schools in the core of the city with white schools in the outlying areas. As described earlier, white students were bused across the river and railroad tracks to inner-city schools, and blacks outward to suburban schools. Thus the plan resembled what might occur if consolidated city/county desegregation took place in a major urban center in the North. To implement the plan, Duval County purchased an additional 150 buses and almost 30,000 students were transported who would have walked to school otherwise. Most of the distances involved were relatively short, but some students traveled up to sixty miles round-trip from home to school and back. Nearly all of the districts' 142 school centers were affected by the plan.

Since blacks constituted less than 50 percent of the school population in each of the districts, a reasonable measure of desegregation effort would be change in the percentage of black students attending schools in which they comprised a minority. An increase in desegregation should mean an increase in the percentage of black students in majority white schools.

Table 2–2
Racial Balances in Schools, 1968–72

		Blacks Attending Public Schools Which Were			
		0–49.9% Black	*50–79.9% Black*	*80–100% Black*	*N*
Dade	1968	16.90%	3.04%	80.06%	56,518
	1970	35.82	32.81	31.37	60,957
	1972	43.71	28.60	27.69	62,558
Duval	1968	12.57	—	87.43	34,638
	1970	24.80	14.75	60.45	36,054
	1972	76.83	9.28	13.89	34,597
Escambia	1968	22.37	6.22	71.41	12,924
	1970	47.55	35.18	17.27	13,443
	1972	46.08	39.53	14.39	13,436
Lee	1968	23.09	1.69	75.22	3,369
	1970	100.00	—	—	3,782
	1972	100.00	—	—	4,300
Leon	1968	35.64	—	64.36	7,183
	1970	81.01	12.82	6.17	7,295
	1972	77.84	17.33	4.83	7,076
Manatee	1968	28.39	0.30	71.31	3,981
	1970	81.39	18.61	—	4,094
	1972	85.46	14.54	—	3,859
Palm Beach	1968	19.25	1.93	78.82	17,158
	1970	30.30	20.10	40.60	18,338
	1972	69.33	26.25	5.02	18,685

Sources: U.S. Department of Health, Education and Welfare, Office of Civil Rights, *Directory of Public Elementary and Secondary Schools in Selected Districts: Enrollment and Staff by Racial/Ethnic Group, Fall, 1968, 1970 and 1972.*

These figures are summarized in table 2–2. As we can see, in each of the districts the implementation of desegregation led to a substantial decline in the percentage of black students in their own schools, and a corresponding increase in black attendance at white schools.

The third column of the table represents the degree of isolation of black students in schools that were all black or nearly so. As the figures for 1968 show, substantial racial isolation existed in all the districts prior to implementation of the court-ordered plan. On average, 80 percent of the black students attended schools that were 80–100 percent black, ranging from a low of 64 percent of the black students in Leon County to a high of 87 percent in Duval County. By 1972, after desegregation was implemented in all the districts, only 18 percent of the black students overall remained racially isolated, almost all of them in the three counties of Dade, Escambia, and Duval.

As the first column in the table shows, the court-ordered plans resulted in an immediate increase in the percentage of black students attending majority white schools. Prior to desegregation (1968) only 18 percent of the black students in the seven districts attended majority white schools. After desegregation (1972) 63 percent did so. In Lee County, racial isolation of black students was eliminated entirely. Top-heavy majorities of black students were assigned to majority white schools in Manatee, Leon, Duval, and Palm Beach Counties. Only in Dade and Escambia Counties did a majority of black students continue to attend majority black schools after the implementation of desegregation.

Desegregation was accompanied by a considerable increase in student transportation. Table 2–3 shows busing rates before and after desegregation for the four districts for whom complete information was available. In three of the cases, the percentage of students transported to public school was substantially higher after implementation of the plan than before. Only in Leon County did the rate decrease somewhat. However, by 1972 the busing rate in Leon had climbed back to the predesegregation level, largely because parents requested bus transportation for elementary children who otherwise would have walked to school in congested traffic zones.

Moreover, the comprehensiveness of desegregation was directly related to the amount of student transportation involved. The districts were ranked from high to low in terms of both variables for the school year 1972–73. The measure for degree of desegregation was the percentage of black students attending majority white schools in each of the districts. Amount of busing was measured by the percentage of all students in each district transported to school at public expense. Lee and Manatee Counties had the greatest degree of desegregation and the highest incidence of busing. Dade County ranked lowest on both measures. The rankings on

Table 2–3
Busing Rates Before and After Implementation of Desegregation

County	*% of Students Transported at Public Expense before Implementation; Year*	*% of Students Transported at Public Expense after Implementation; Year*
Duval	26.82%, 1970	44.64%, 1972
Escambia	44.98%, 1968	52.79%, 1969
Leon	45.83%, 1969	41.83%, 1970
Palm Beach	28.92%, 1970	40.06%, 1971

Sources: U.S. Commission on Civil Rights, *The Diminishing Barrier: A Report on School Desegregation in Nine Communities* (Washington, D.C., 1972); State of Florida, Department of Education, *Profiles of Florida School Districts, 1970–74.*

both indicators were reasonably consistent for Leon, Duval, and Palm Beach Counties. Only Escambia County was "out of place," so to speak, ranking sixth on the measure of desegregation but third on incidence of busing, doubtless because Escambia County provided transportation for elementary and middle school students who lived less than two miles from school, whereas the other districts for the most part transported only those students residing beyond a two-mile radius from the nearest school. The rank-order correlation (Spearman's Rho) between desegregation and busing for the seven districts was .79, indicating a high relationship between the two.[47] Despite the fact that only two counties employed what were avowedly called "busing" plans to desegregate, these findings confirm Foster's observation that comprehensive desegregation planning, by whatever name, necessitates additional transportation.[48]

The Private School Movement

With the advent of public school desegregation, Florida provided fertile soil for private school development. The state already possessed one of the stronger private school traditions in the South. In 1960, long before desegregation was achieved, about 8 percent of the white elementary and secondary students in Florida attended private schools, compared to an average of 6 percent in the rest of the South.[49]

Enrollment data give strong evidence that public school desegregation in Florida was accompanied by private school avoidance. Statewide, private school enrollments increased approximately 16 percent from 1969–73, considerably above the public school enrollment increase of 8.6 percent for the same period.[50] In our seven districts, the Florida Educational Directory reported a total of 200 private schools in 1970–71. By 1973–74 that figure had grown to 290, an increase of 45 percent.[51]

Table 2–4 compares private and public school enrollment growth rates for the seven districts from 1970–73. Overall, the private school rate exceeded the public school rate by a considerable margin. Private school enrollments increased by more than 34 percent, while public school enrollments grew by less than 2 percent. Private school avoidance appeared particularly strong in Leon and Duval Counties and was considerable in Dade and Palm Beach as well. While public school growth exceeded private school growth in Lee and Manatee, private school growth was still appreciable in both counties.

There is little doubt that private school growth occurred at the expense of the public schools, as indicated by a reasonably strong rank order correlation (Spearman's Rho) of .64 between high private versus

Table 2–4
Comparison of Private and Public School Enrollment Growth, K–12, 1970–73

	Number of Students					
	Private		*Public*		*% Change*	
County	*1970*	*1973*	*1970*	*1973*	*Private*	*Public*
Leon	1,482	2,766	22,376	22,816	+86.64	+ 1.97
Duval	8,777	14,179	130,680	121,118	+61.55	− 7.32
Dade	33,138	44,306	259,452	263,932	+33.70	+ 1.73
Palm Beach	7,195	9,081	74,380	77,542	+26.21	+ 4.25
Manatee	744	840	18,585	21,609	+12.90	+16.27
Lee	1,044	1,168	23,350	30,018	+11.88	+28.56
Escambia	6,205	6,377	51,192	51,815	+ 2.77	+ 1.22
Totals	58,585	78,717	580,041	588,920	+34.36	+ 1.53

Sources: *Florida Statistical Abstract, 1970, 1974; Florida Educational Directory, 1970/71, 1973/74.*

low public growth. Furthermore, private school growth was undoubtedly accounted for virtually entirely by whites. Updated private enrollment figures in the seven counties by school and by race were impossible to obtain. However, 1970 census figures showed that private school enrollment throughout the state was 94 percent white.[52]

To determine what kinds of schools were the beneficiaries of avoidance, private schools in the seven counties were classified into three types: (1) Catholic parochial; (2) Protestant and other sectarian; (3) nonsectarian.[53] In 1970, the majority of private school students (61 percent) attended Catholic parochial schools. By 1973, however, the balance had shifted, with a majority of students (56 percent) attending Protestant and other sectarian or nonsectarian schools. Catholic parochial enrollments actually declined from 1970–73, while enrollments in the other two categories of schools rose sharply. The steadiest and most substantial growth rate occurred in Protestant and other sectarian schools, with enrollments increasing in every county (see table 2–5).

Much of the growth in non-Catholic sectarian schools from 1970–73 was accounted for by so-called "Christian academies," established in direct response to public school desegregation. Often Baptist denominational, these schools developed as white segregation academies combining the three R's with a strong dose of fundamentalist religion.[54]

In Duval County, 71 percent of the reported growth in Protestant school enrollments came from five Christian academies that had opened their doors since 1970.[55] Leon County's two Christian academies doubled

Table 2–5
Private School Enrollments, by Type, 1970–73

	Fall, 1970	*Fall, 1973*	*% Change, 1970–73*
Catholic parochial	N 35,731 % 60.99	N 34,648 % 44.02	− 3.03
Protestant and other sectarian	N 12,526 % 21.38	N 26,445 % 33.60	+111.12
Nonsectarian	N 10,328 % 17.63	N 17,624 % 22.38	+ 70.64
Totals	N 58,585 % 100.00	N 78,717 % 100.00	+ 34.36

Source: *Florida Educational Directory, 1970/71–1973/74.*

in size.[56] Nine academies contributed 51 percent of the growth in Dade County's non-Catholic sectarian schools.[57]

Nonsectarian schools also grew considerably, but more erratically, from 1970–73. In three counties, they actually lost students. In the other four, however, they gained substantially, reaching a peak growth rate of 168 percent in Palm Beach County.[58]

Thus the traditional denominational schools were not the prime beneficiaries of avoidance. To be sure, not all the students enrolled in Catholic, Episcopalian, Lutheran, or Hebrew schools were there exclusively for religious reasons. However, the singular contribution of avoidance to private education was in the creation and growth of schools that would not have existed but for public school desegregation.

While these figures on private schools demonstrate impressive growth, it should be kept in mind that nowhere in the seven districts did avoidance immediately jeopardize the prospects for biracial schooling. The 78,717 students in private schools in 1973 represented 12 percent of all the students in school, a substantial number to be sure but not an overwhelming proportion. Despite the extraordinary private school growth rates, public school enrollments increased in six of the seven counties. While Duval County showed a net loss in public school enrollments, whites still outnumbered blacks in the public schools by a margin of two to one.

The aggregate figures presented in this chapter do not yield many visible clues as to the sources of avoidance. Duval County's desegregation plan involved a substantial increase in busing and was accompanied by substantial private school growth. In Leon County, busing actually decreased with desegregation, yet the rate of private school enrollment growth in that county exceeded Duval's. Private school growth was greater in Dade County than in Palm Beach, yet Dade bused a far smaller percentage of students and a considerable degree of racial imbalance continued in Dade's schools even after the implementation of desegregation. These anomalies add weight to the point made in the first chapter that in order to isolate the factors associated with avoidance we must delve beneath aggregate statistics and explore the phenomenon at the level of its actual occurrence—the individual parental decision-maker.

Notes

1. Bureau of Census, *1972 Census of Governments: Governmental Organization* (Washington, D.C.: U.S. Government Printing Office, 1973), p. 340.
2. Ibid.
3. Clyde F. Snyder, in collaboration with Samuel K. Gove, *American State and Local Government,* 2d ed. (New York: Appleton-Century-Crofts, 1965), pp. 548–49.
4. Marilyn Gittell, "School Desegregation and the Courts," *Social Policy,* 6 (January/February 1976), 38.
5. *Florida Constitution, 1885,* Article 12, Section 12.
6. *Mims et al.* v. *Duval County School Board et al.,* U.S. District Court, Middle District of Florida, Jacksonville District, No. 4598-Civ-J, p. 2.
7. Reed Sarratt, *The Ordeal of Desegregation* (New York: Harper and Row, 1966), pp. 35–36, 115–18.
8. Ibid., pp. 8–10.
9. Ibid., p. 359.
10. The role of federal agencies under the Civil Rights Act of 1964 is discussed in U.S. Commission on Civil Rights, *Twenty Years After Brown: Equality of Educational Opportunity* (Washington, D.C.: 1975), pp. 10–23.
11. U.S. Department of Health, Education and Welfare, Office for Civil Rights, *Directory of Public Elementary and Secondary Schools in Selected Districts: Enrollment and Staff by Racial/Ethnic Group, Fall, 1972* (Washington, D.C.: U.S. Government Printing Office), pp. 230–53.
12. Ralph B. Thompson, ed., *Florida Statistical Abstract, 1973* (Gainesville, Fla.: University of Florida Press, 1973), p. 34.
13. Ibid.
14. U.S. Commission on Civil Rights, *Twenty Years After Brown,* p. 56.
15. U.S. Department of Health, Education and Welfare, *Directory of Public Elementary and Secondary Schools in Selected Districts, Fall,*

1972, p. 234; Ralph B. Thompson, ed., *Florida Statistical Abstract, 1974* (Gainesville, Fla.: University of Florida Press, 1974), p. 87.

16. Sarratt, *Ordeal of Desegregation,* p. 99.

17. Ibid.

18. U.S. Department of Health, Education and Welfare, Office for Civil Rights, *Directory of Public Elementary and Secondary Schools in Selected Districts: Enrollment and Staff by Racial/Ethnic Groups, Fall, 1968* (Washington, D.C.: U.S. Government Printing Office), pp. 239–41.

19. For a full review of desegregation planning techniques see Gordon Foster, ''Desegregating Urban Schools: A Review of Techniques,'' *Harvard Educational Review,* 43 (February 1973), 5–36.

20. *Florida Statistical Abstract, 1974,* p. 87; HEW, *Directory of Public Elementary and Secondary Schools, Fall, 1972,* p. 237; U.S. Civil Rights Commission, *Twenty Years After Brown,* p. 56.

21. The initial suit was titled *Brafton et al.,* v. *The Board of Public Instruction of Duval County, Florida, et al.*

22. *Mims* v. *Duval County,* p. 5.

23. HEW, *Directory of Public Elementary and Secondary Schools, Fall, 1968,* pp. 242–43.

24. See Micheal W. Giles, ''Racial Stability and Urban School Desegregation,'' *Urban Affairs Quarterly,* 12 (June 1977), 499–510.

25. An additional 150 buses were purchased to implement the plan and nearly 30,000 students were transported who otherwise would have walked to school.

26. *Florida Statistical Abstract, 1973,* pp. 36–37.

27. *Florida Statistical Abstract, 1974,* p. 88; U.S. Civil Rights Commission, *Twenty Years After Brown,* p. 57; HEW, *Directory of Public Elementary and Secondary Schools, Fall, 1972,* p. 249.

28. HEW, *Directory of Public Elementary and Secondary Schools, Fall, 1968,* pp. 252–53.

29. See Micheal W. Giles, Douglas S. Gatlin, and Everett F. Cataldo, *Determinants of Resegregation: Compliance/Rejection Behavior and Policy Alternatives.* Final report submitted to National Science Foundation, June 1976, p. II–3.

30. *Florida Statistical Abstract, 1973,* p. 34.

31. Ibid.

32. *Florida Statistical Abstract, 1974,* p. 87.

33. U.S. Commission on Civil Rights, *The Diminishing Barrier: A Report on School Desegregation in Nine Communities* (Washington, D.C.: 1972), pp. 11–12.

34. *Florida Statistical Abstract, 1973,* p. 36.

35. *Florida Statistical Abstract, 1974,* p. 88; HEW, *Directory of Public Elementary and Secondary Schools, Fall, 1972,* p. 243.

36. U.S. Civil Rights Commission, *The Diminishing Barrier,* p. 45.
37. Ibid., pp. 45–46.
38. *Florida Statistical Abstract, 1973,* p. 35.
39. *Florida Statistical Abstract, 1974,* p. 87; HEW, *Directory of Public Elementary and Secondary Schools, Fall, 1972,* p. 242.
40. Giles, Gatlin, and Cataldo, *Determinants of Resegregation,* p. II–3.
41. *Florida Statistical Abstract, 1973,* p. 36.
42. *Florida Statistical Abstract, 1974,* p. 88; HEW, *Directory of Public Elementary and Secondary Schools, Fall, 1972,* p. 244.
43. Giles, Gatlin, and Cataldo, *Determinants of Resegregation,* p. II–3.
44. *Florida Statistical Abstract, 1974,* pp. 3, 86.
45. U.S. Department of Health, Education and Welfare, Office for Civil Rights, *Directory of Public Elementary and Secondary Schools in Selected Districts: Enrollment and Staff by Racial/Ethnic Group, Fall, 1970* (Washington, D.C.: U.S. Government Printing Office), pp. 255–56.
46. *Florida Statistical Abstract,* 1974, p. 131.
47. William Buchanan, *Understanding Political Variables* (New York: Charles Scribner's Sons, 1969), pp. 214–16.
48. Foster, "Desegregating Urban Schools," p. 31.
49. Bureau of Census, *Statistical Abstract of the United States, 1963* (Washington, D.C.: U.S. Government Printing Office, 1963), p. 131.
50. Florida Department of Education, *Florida Educational Directory for 1969/70–73/74* (Tallahassee, Fla.: Department of Education).
51. Department of Education, *Florida Educational Directory, 1970–71,* pp. 223–56; *Florida Educational Directory, 1973–74,* pp. 218–57.
52. Bureau of Census, *U.S. Census of Population: General Social and Economic Characteristics, 1970* (Washington, D.C.: U.S. Government Printing Office, 1972), Florida, Section 2, pp. 629–50.
53. Information on affiliation is contained in the *Florida Educational Directory.*
54. See David Nevin and Robert Bills, *The Schools That Fear Built* (Washington, D.C.: Acropolis Books, 1976).
55. Department of Education, *Florida Educational Directory, 1970–71,* pp. 236–39; *Florida Educational Directory, 1973–74,* p. 245.
56. Department of Education, *Florida Educational Directory, 1970–71,* p. 244; *Florida Educational Directory, 1973–74,* p. 245.
57. Department of Education, *Florida Educational Directory, 1970–71,* pp. 228–36; *Florida Educational Directory, 1973–74,* pp. 223–36.
58. Department of Education, *Florida Educational Directory, 1970–71,* pp. 248–50; *Florida Educational Directory, 1973–74,* pp. 249–51.

3 Data and Methods

The following chapters are based on extensive interviews conducted in the 1972–73 school year with parents of school children in the seven counties. Two sets of respondents were delineated: (1) compliers—parents whose children remained in the public schools to which they were assigned by the desegregation plan; and (2) avoiders—parents who withdrew their children from assigned public schools and placed them in local private schools.

Sampling Procedures

Official school district records provided the basic sampling frame. Each district maintained pupil locator files or computer listings for each student in the school system with information including the name of the child, assigned public school, grade, race, sex, address, telephone number, and name of the household head. In each district, this information was compiled on a card systematically for every "nth" student (the interval varied according to the number of students in district schools) having attended public schools in both 1971–72 and 1972–73. Eliminating siblings, a list was thereby produced from which the complier sampler was chosen at random.

Official records also contained information on student transfers and withdrawals which was used as the basis for the avoider sample. In each district we recorded the names of all students identified by a uniform statewide code as having switched from a public school in the district to a private school in the county between 1971–72 and 1972–73. In four districts where transfer records were incomplete, visits were made to all sizable private schools in the county to request information on students who had entered in 1972–73. In most cases, the private schools agreed to supply the names of such students along with the names of their parents, addresses, and telephone numbers. By telephone screening, we retained the names of those students who had transferred after attending public schools in the county in 1971–72. The combined lists from public and private schools constituted the sampling frame for avoiders. In some districts interviews were sought with all identified avoiders; in other districts, with longer lists, random sampling was employed.

In one county, access to official public school records was denied.

Complier interviews were obtained on the basis of an area probability sample, with blocks chosen at random from census tract data. These blocks were canvassed and interviews were obtained in households with public school children. Avoiders were identified from lists provided by nine of the largest private schools in the county. Again, compliers were classified as those parents whose children attended public schools for both 1971–72 and 1972–73; avoiders, as those parents whose children were transferred from a public school in 1971–72 to a private school in 1972–73.

Each interview with an adult respondent was conducted with respect to a specific "cue" child identified from the public or private school lists in all cases except the area probability county in which the "cue" child for compliers was selected randomly from among all public school children in each household. Where both parents were present within the household, respondents were selected on a random basis.

The samples for Duval, Leon, Escambia, Manatee, and Lee Counties were drawn during fall 1972. The samples in Dade and Palm Beach were drawn in winter 1973. Interviews were conducted in winter-spring 1973.

Sample Description

Table 3–1 reveals a very close match between the school grade distributions of "cue" children in our sample and all public and private school students in the seven counties. Among compliers, 49.4 percent of the children attended elementary schools, very close to the figure of 51.1 percent in elementary grades for all public school students in the counties.

Table 3–1
School Attendance Figures in Seven Counties, 1972–73

	Sample of Compliers	*All Public School Students*	*Sample of Avoiders*	*All Private School Students*
		Elementary Grades (1–6)		
N	1,043	296,548	797	44,183
%	49.4	51.1	57.5	59.0
		Secondary Grades (7–12)		
N	1,069	283,781	589	30,703
%	50.6	48.9	42.5	41.0

Source: Ralph B. Thompson, ed., *Florida Statistical Abstract, 1974* (Gainesville, Fla.: University of Florida Press, 1974).

At the secondary level, 48.9 percent of all the school children were in grades 7–12, compared to 50.6 percent for our complier sample. The figures for avoiders are equally close: 57.5 percent of the avoider sample had children in private elementary schools with the remaining 42.5 percent in secondary schools. Among all private school students in the seven counties, the comparable figures were 59 percent and 41 percent, respectively. Thus, a very close correspondence exists between sample statistics and population parameters for both public and private school enrollments.

The analyses in Chapters 4, 5, and 6 are based on these samples of compliers and avoiders. In addition, a sample of black compliers was also drawn in the seven counties. Their responses are analyzed and contrasted with those of white parents in Chapter 6.

Sources of Data

The survey instrument contained numerous items relating to the public schools respondents' children attended in 1971–72; the schools attended in 1972–73 (public for compliers, private for avoiders); and the public schools avoiders children were assigned to attend in 1972–73 under the desegregation plans. Information was sought from respondents on such matters as busing, racial balances in the schools, condition of schools and neighborhoods in which they were located, status of the schools before desegregation, safety and discipline within the schools, satisfaction with quality of education. On many of the same items, objective measures were obtained from official sources—state and local units of government and U.S. Census data.

The instrument also contained items on the personal characteristics of respondents, sources of information on school desegregation, participation in school affairs, and attitudes on a variety of issues. The instrument underwent several informal pretests and then was pretested formally with a random sample of respondents in a Florida county that was not included among the research sites. At each pretest stage, items were checked for validity and reliability, clarity and responses effectiveness, and several revisions were made prior to the actual fieldwork. The final instrument contained nearly 200 items and took approximately ninety minutes to administer.

Fieldwork

The survey was conducted by National Analysts, Inc., of Philadelphia. All interviews were conducted by experienced professionals from National Analysts' Florida field staff, working directly under local supervision with overall field coordination by staff from the Philadelphia office. Extensive training sessions for interviewers were held throughout the seven counties under supervision of National Analysts' staff and the coauthors. Respondents and interviewers were matched by race. Interviews were checked directly for authenticity by field supervisors in each of the counties.

All interviews were conducted personally with respondents in their homes, with anonymity and confidentiality guaranteed. Most of the interviews were obtained at initial contact. For those that were not, up to three callbacks were routinely made. The overall response rate was 84 percent: by respondent group, 88 percent for compliers, 76 percent for avoiders.

In addition to the large survey conducted in 1973, follow-up interviews were conducted a year later with a subsample (N = 1,000) of the original respondents. Responses from the second survey appear selectively in Chapters 4–6.

4 The Avoiders: Who Are They?

As we have just seen, avoidance was not rampant in the seven Florida counties. From a quantitative standpoint, therefore, our findings parallel more closely those of Rossell and Farley than of Coleman. Avoidance, however, has important qualitative aspects as well. If withdrawal occurs mostly among higher-status families, then an important leadership stratum is lost to the public schools. Furthermore, school desegregation is a policy of class as well as race. Few advocates of desegregation would suggest that placing lower-class white and black students in the same schools will enhance the education or socialization experience of either group.

On the other hand, if avoidance stems largely from racial hostility and prejudice, then it may actually have some therapeutic effects by removing a source of racial tension from the schools and easing the task of making desegregation work. Thus to assess the impact of avoidance it is important to know who leaves as well as how many.

Social Status and Avoidance

Higher social status is commonly associated with greater tolerance on racial issues.[1] Melvin M. Tumin found that attitudinal readiness to accept desegregation increased with social status.[2] Thomas F. Pettigrew and Robert L. Crain found that desegregation was achieved more quickly in relatively prosperous school districts.[3] From these findings we might assume that upper-status parents are more receptive to desegregation and less likely to transfer their children to private schools.

However, there is contrary evidence that, despite their greater avowed racial tolerance, higher-status families are in fact more likely to withdraw from biracial stiuations. Out-migration from desegregated neighborhoods seems to be rooted in class norms. Higher-class families tend to have more favorable attitudes toward neighborhood integration, but move, nevertheless, for reasons of status concerns and conformity with perceived peer-group expectations.[4] The same kind of "classist" phenomenon may exist with respect to withdrawal from desegregated schools. As status increases, so may the concerns individuals have about their "image" if they leave their children in school with lower-status blacks, and their feeling that maintenance of social respectability requires withdrawal.

On the practical side, placing a child in a private school is an expensive alternative to compliance. While the tuition cost of private schools is in some cases as low as $500/year, this still constitutes a heavy financial burden for lower-income families.[5] Thus, quite apart from the issue of attitudinal tolerance, upper-class, higher-income families have a greater opportunity to choose the private school alternative than do lower-class, lower-income individuals.

Are avoiders in our seven Florida school districts distinguished from compliers in terms of their social status? The answer to this question is clearly affirmative. This difference is most dramatic in the area of income. The median income for an avoiding family in our sample was almost $17,000 a year. By comparison compliers had a median income of only slightly more than $12,000 a year. As the distributions in table 4–1 indicate, the disparity was greatest at the highest income levels. Almost 25 percent of the avoiding families had an income in excess of $24,000 a year while this was true for only about 7 percent of the complying families. These results are consistent with Charles T. Clotfelter's finding that private school enrollment growth in seventy-eight Mississippi counties was directly related to the percent of the population earning more than $25,000 a year.[6]

Table 4–1
Social Status and Avoidance

	% *Compliers*	% *Avoiders*
Income		
Less than $9,000	26.2	9.8
$9,000–$11,999	21.5	12.4
$12,000–$14,999	18.4	16.8
$15,000–$17,999	13.5	16.4
$18,000–$20,999	8.8	11.5
$21,000–$23,999	4.2	9.0
$24,000 and over	7.4	24.1
Education		
Grades 0–8	11.0	4.7
Grades 9–12	63.6	51.0
College	25.4	44.3
Occupational Prestige[a]		
Low	12.4	5.4
Medium	29.1	20.1
High	58.4	74.5

[a]Based on Duncan SEI. See Otis D. Duncan, "A Socioeconomic Index for All Occupations," in Albert J. Reiss, ed., *Occupation and Social Status* (New York: Free Press, 1961), chap. 6 and appendix B.

The contrast between compliers and avoiders was nearly as dramatic in terms of their education and occupation. The median school years completed for both compliers and avoiders was approximately twelve (12.45 for compliers and 12.85 for avoiders). But almost 45 percent of the avoiders had attended college as compared to only about 25 percent of the compliers. Similarly, 75 percent of the avoiders had high-prestige occupations compared to only 58 percent of the compliers. Thus on average avoiders appear to be higher in social status than compliers. They have more education, more prestigious occupations, and earn more money. Income represents the greatest difference between the two groups, signifying the importance of financial resources to avoidance behavior.

Religious Affiliation

Many religious groups maintained schools prior to desegregation. The onset of desegregation, however, served as a catalyst for the growth of denominational schools in the South. The growth was particularly pronounced among the more fundamentalist Protestant sects, many of whom were already leaning toward the establishment of their own schools because of the Supreme Court's decision removing religious observances and instruction from the public schools. When the schools became not only godless but desegregated as well, the commitment to private, "Bible-based" schools was made.[7]

As expected, fundamentalist religions were well represented among avoiders. Approximately 40 percent of them indicated that they were members of either the Baptist or Methodist churches. The fundamentalist sects, however, were even better represented among the compliers, 50 percent of whom reported they were either Baptist or Methodist. About 20 percent of the avoiders belonged to the Lutheran, Presbyterian, and Episcopal churches, compared to about 14 percent of the compliers, reflecting the generally higher status of avoiding families. It should also be noted that avoiders were more likely than compliers to be Roman Catholics (19 percent versus 14 percent), despite the fact that the Catholic Church stood steadfastly against its schools becoming havens from desegregation.

Thus while private schools affiliated with fundamentalist churches have grown dramatically, avoidance is not confined to a particular religious sect. Furthermore, the presence of an existing system of parochial schools may lure members of that faith from the public schools.

Regional Origin

The South's experiences with slavery, the Civil War, and Reconstruction have long separated that region from the mainstream of America on racial issues. Southerners have consistently been found to possess more hostile attitudes toward blacks than nonsoutherners.[8] Support for racist candidates, lynchings, job and voting discrimination have all occurred more frequently in the South than elsewhere. While the last two decades have brought remarkable changes to the South, there is ample evidence to suggest that regional differences in attitudes persist. For example, in a recent report from the National Opinion Research Center, Andrew Greeley and Paul B. Sheatsley indicated that while acceptance of the principle of integrated education has increased in the South over the years, southern whites remained behind nonsouthern whites in their level of acceptance.[9] Similarly, in a recent analysis of Gallup survey data for the years 1965 and 1970, Melvin J. Knapp and Jon P. Alston reported that southerners expressed greater resistance than nonsoutherners to school desegregation in both years.[10] The apparently greater acceptance of school desegregation outside the South seems belied, however, by recent resistance to desegregation in several nonsouthern areas.

Florida has experienced considerable inmigration from other southern states and from the Northeast. In 1970, approximately two-thirds of Florida's population had been born outside of the state.[11] This pattern of migration also appears among our respondents. Approximately 40 percent of the persons interviewed indicated that they were reared outside of the South. We might expect that these respondents, coming from a more racially tolerant environment where legal segregation of the races had not been practiced, would be overrepresented among complying parents. Given their cultural heritage we would expect avoiders to be disproportionately from the South. This anticipated pattern, however, did not emerge. Southerners (from or reared in Ala., Ark., Fla., Ga., La., Miss., S.C., N.C., Tenn., Tex., Va.) constituted approximately 60 percent of the compliers and about 55 percent of the avoiders. Given that nonsouthern migrants tended to have slightly higher incomes than southerners, the larger number of nonsouthern respondents among the avoiders is partially attributable to their greater ability to afford private school rather than to the presence of psychological or subcultural attributes. In any case, these results confirm that avoidance of desegregation is not a distinctly southern phenomenon.

Attitudes and Avoidance

Racial Prejudice

Resistance to school desegregation is widely assumed to be a product of racial prejudice.[12] This view is supported by a lengthy research tradition indicating a relationship between antiblack behavior and racial prejudice.[13] Attempts to examine the relationship between racial prejudice and resistance to school desegregation, however, have been limited. In one such attempt, Tumin found a relationship between racial attitudes and readiness to accept school desegregation.[14] Tumin was predicting from one attitude scale to another, and even then found "variability and inconsistency." However, in light of Tumin's findings and the strength of scholarly and nonscholarly opinion, we would expect avoiders to be more racially prejudiced than compliers.

The data presented in table 4–2 provide little support for this widespread expectation. Avoiders were slightly more likely than compliers to think stereotypically that blacks have less respect for law and order and that whites take better care of their children; but, in general, the differences between avoiders and compliers on the racial prejudice items were minuscule.

Class Prejudice

While most research has focused on racial prejudice to explain discrimination, Hubert Blalock has suggested that class prejudice may be at work instead. The concept of class prejudice is based on the assumption that persons prefer to interact with others of equal or higher social status.[15] According to James M. Beshers, status hierarchies tend to be self-maintaining through time because higher-ranking groups impose status inequalities upon lower-ranking groups.[16] Status inequalities consist largely of behavioral norms that delimit the scope and content of interaction between the higher and lower classes. Accordingly, "status sensitive" people are likely to be found in higher statuses and are concerned with maximizing the social distance between themselves and those of lower status. This tendency of higher-status groups to regulate their social interaction with lower-status groups is particularly evident within major institutional settings, which would include the public schools.

Because blacks continue to cluster toward the bottom of the status hierarchy, desegregation results not only in an influx of black children into the white child's environment but also an influx of predominantly lower-class children into an essentially middle-class environment. Consequently school desegregation jeopardizes the maintenance of status inequalities as it increases opportunities for social relations between higher- and lower-status children. Thus, while avoiders are not more racially prejudiced than compliers they may be more class prejudiced and less willing to have their children in the mixed-class situation that desegregation creates.

The concept of class prejudice embodies the idea of avoiding interac-

Table 4–2
Attitudes and Avoidance

		% Agree	% Neither	% Disagree
Racial Prejudice				
1. In general, black people have less respect for	C	60.0	5.0	35.1
law and order than white people do.	A	64.0	4.6	31.5
2. In general, white parents take better care of	C	52.8	8.4	38.7
their children than black parents do.	A	55.3	7.3	37.3
3. Knowing that a person is black tells you a lot	C	18.8	2.9	78.3
about what to expect from him.	A	17.0	2.5	80.5
Class Prejudice				
1. Live in your town.	C	96.9	2.0	1.1
	A	94.2	3.3	2.5
2. Live in your end of town.	C	94.0	2.4	3.6
	A	89.0	3.2	7.9
3. Live in your neighborhood.	C	88.8	2.5	8.7
	A	80.2	3.6	16.2
4. Live across the street.	C	86.4	2.5	11.1
	A	76.3	3.8	19.9
5. Live in the same apartment building.	C	84.6	3.1	12.3
	A	77.5	4.0	18.5
Attitude toward School Integration				
1. Schools ought to be integrated to help black and	C	56.7	2.9	40.4
white children understand each other better.	A	55.5	2.5	42.0
2. Different races will get along better some day	C	66.1	3.6	30.3
if they all go to school together now.	A	62.3	3.8	34.0
3. School integration will help give black chil-	C	46.4	3.5	50.1
dren the rights they should have had all along.	A	45.4	3.7	50.9
Legitimacy of School Desegregation Policy				
1. The government has no right to tell you	C	83.3	1.9	14.8
where to send your child to school.	A	87.1	1.2	11.7
2. The Supreme Court doesn't have any busi-	C	62.7	4.0	33.3
ness making decisions about school integration.	A	63.5	2.5	34.0
Efficacy				
1. People like you don't have any say about	C	47.8	1.6	50.7
what the government does.	A	50.3	1.1	48.6
2. Sometimes politics and government seem so	C	74.8	.8	24.5
complicated that a person like you really can't understand what is going on.	A	72.8	.4	26.8
3. You don't think that public officials care	C	57.0	1.8	41.1
much what people like you think.	A	55.6	2.2	42.3

C = compliers; A = avoiders.

tion with lower-status persons by maintaining a considerable degree of social distance. Most studies of social distance have provided an ethnic group (for example, Jew, Armenian, Negro) or an occupational group (for example, janitor, mechanic, plumber) as an object of social distance. To invoke the image of a lower-status object, our respondents were presented with the following brief description of a hypothetical family which included occupational, educational, and income elements which were objectively lower class:

Mr. Smith is a white janitor at the high school. His wife is a cafeteria worker. They both quit school before the eighth grade. The family's yearly income is six thousand five hundred dollars.

The respondents were then asked a series of questions about their willingness to let the Smith family live in varying degrees of proximity to themselves.[17] The responses to these questions are presented in table 4–2.

In general, neither compliers nor avoiders exhibited a high degree of class prejudice. Even where the question involved close residential proximity (for example, living in the same apartment building) more than three-fourths of both groups responded affirmatively. However, consistent differences existed between compliers and avoiders, particularly where the questions involved the neighborhood or closer. For each of these questions avoiders were about 7 to 10 percent less positive than compliers. Thus, while class prejudice was not strong in either group, avoiders were somewhat more likely than compliers to exhibit it.

Attitude toward School Integration

While racial attitudes do not distinguish compliers and avoiders, we would imagine negative attitudes toward school integration to be more common among avoiders than compliers. The responses to three items dealing with the goals of school integration are shown in table 4–2. Contrary to expectations, the distribution of responses for compliers and avoiders on these three items is virtually identical. Both groups were equally likely to see school integration as promoting racial harmony and giving black children the rights they should have had all along. This same pattern was exhibited when the respondents were asked simply, "How do you feel about school integration?" Almost 49 percent of the compliers responded that they approved strongly or approved. For avoiders approval was only slightly less, at 46 percent.

While avoiders and compliers appear to be undifferentiated in their general attitudes toward desegregation, they may differ in their attitudes toward the way in which it was implemented. To examine this possibility, respondents were asked, "How do you feel about the way school desegregation was handled around here?" Approximately 75 percent of the avoiders disapproved of the handling of desegregation compared to approximately 60 percent of the compliers. Thus, both groups of respondents were more negative about the way school desegregation was implemented than about school desegregation in principle, and avoiders were considerably more negative than compliers about implementation.

The respondents cited numerous reasons for their disapproval of the handling of desegregation, but the largest single group of responses clustered around the issue of busing. Approximately 30 percent of all disapproving respondents cited some aspect of busing as their reason. While avoiders were more likely to disapprove of the way desegregation was handled, they were about as likely as compliers to mention busing as the cause of their opposition. The following quotations illustrate typical responses focusing on busing:

Respondent #150160:
I don't believe in busing. I think it should be a neighborhood school concept, period. . . . I do believe in integration. I wish that our private school would integrate.

Respondent #550021:
I can't see busing children from one end of town to the other when they have a school close by. School buses raise taxes.

Respondent #850289:
I think a child spending too much time on a bus is bad.

Respondent #850179:
I think it's wrong to take a child out of his area and bused to another. Children need to be closer to home.

Respondent #973002:
. . . Each child should go to the neighborhood school to spend more time studying instead of traveling on buses.

As might be expected, objections to busing were symbolic of a wide number of complaints. These included long distances and time, and fears about bus safety and the security of the area where the school was located. What it all amounts to at the verbal level, however, is opposition to the principle of achieving racial balance through busing. And, as the first quoted response indicates, this opposition was (at least in the parents' minds) distinct from opposition to school integration *per se*. A study by Jonathan Kelley using national survey data has also found attitudes about busing to be distinguishable from attitudes about race and school desegregation.[18]

The second most frequently mentioned reason for disapproving of the way in which school desegregation had been implemented involved its involuntary nature. Approximately 24 percent of both groups cited this reason. The following quotations typify responses about "force":

Respondent #850384:
I don't believe in forced integration. I strongly believe in individual rights. Anybody should be able to do what they want as long as it doesn't hurt anybody else.

Respondent #760871:
We are not given a choice. We are told we have to send them to integrated schools.

Respondent #250452:
I don't feel the parents have any choice as to what schools the children go to.

These responses clearly reflect American ideas of individual liberty and the strong appeal of "freedom of choice." As the history of school desegregation graphically illustrates, however, when given a choice, white parents chose white schools.

Approximately 9 percent of disapproving avoiders and compliers cited the pace of desegregation as a reason:

Respondent #150183:
I think that the big jump from total segregation to total integration has just caused chaos.

Respondent #650010:
Since integration was inevitable, it could have been done more gradually. . . . Also integration should have been started with younger children instead of older ones.

Respondent #150040:
It was pushed on everybody too fast. . . . I guess we weren't ready to accept it, but then we probably never would be.

Clearly, the parents would have preferred a more gradual approach to school desegregation than they experienced. Of course, when gradualism was being accepted by the courts, school districts refused to desegregate at all. Perhaps, as the third respondent suggests, we are never really ready for changes of such magnitude, and never welcome them fully when they finally come.

Thus, compliers and avoiders are indistinguishable in terms of their attitudes toward desegregation generally and its goals. Avoiders, however, are more disapproving of the way that school desegregation has been implemented. But the reasons for their disapproval are the same as those given by compliers who disapprove: busing, force, and speed.

Legitimacy of Desegregation Policy

It has been asserted that compliance with a policy is influenced by perceptions of the legitimacy of the policymaker.[19] The issue of legitimacy turns on whether people think that the policymaker is endowed with the moral authority to make particular decisions. According to this line of reasoning, where policymakers are not perceived to be legitimate, the willingness to accede to their policies should decrease. The frequent mention of "force" as a reason for disapproving of the way school desegregation was implemented suggests that the legitimacy of desegregation might be in question among significant numbers of our respondents.

An examination of the distributions in table 4–2 confirms this possibility. More than 80 percent of all respondents did not believe that the government has a right to tell them where to send their child to school. Similarly, more than 60 percent did not believe that the Supreme Court even has a right to be making decisions about school desegregation. These items distinguished compliers from avoiders hardly at all.

Efficacy

Guidelines on how to desegregate the schools have commonly emphasized parental involvement in desegregation planning. Al Smith, Anthony Downs, and M. Leanne Lachman, for example, have asserted that "school administrators should attempt to actively involve as many people as possible in the school desegregation process. The process of meaningful involvement by community members produces support for the school and for what they are trying to accomplish. Such support is essential for the achievement of effective desegregation."[20] If a sense of participation or influence is conducive to support, we would expect avoiders to have a lower sense of efficacy than compliers. As the data in table 4–2 reveal, compliers and avoiders were about equally likely to believe that they do not have a say in government and that government is too difficult to understand. Of course, since efficacy normally increases with social status and since avoiders have a higher social status than compliers, the fact that the two groups do not differ suggests that the perceived ability to influence government is lower among avoiders than it should be.

Trust

Closely related to the concept of efficacy is that of trust. The concept of trust focuses on individual support and evaluation of governmental actors. As table 4–3 shows, avoiders are less trusting of school officials. While more than half of the compliers thought they could just about always trust school officials to do what is right, only 44 percent of the avoiders felt that way. While compliers and avoiders may not differ in the

Table 4–3
Trust and Avoidance

	% *Compliers*	% *Avoiders*
1. How much of the time do you think you can trust the local school officials to do what is right?		
a. just about always	9.1	7.5
b. most of the time	43.2	36.1
c. some of the time	40.9	48.7
d. almost never	6.8	7.7
2. Would you say that the local schools are		
a. pretty much run by a few big interests	35.6	42.4
b. run for the benefit of all	64.4	57.6
3. Do you feel that		
a. almost all of the officials running the local schools are smart people who usually know what they're doing	66.0	61.9
b. do you think that most of them don't seem to know what they're doing	34.0	38.1
4. Do you think that the local schools		
a. waste a lot of money we pay in taxes	32.5	42.3
b. some of it	50.5	43.4
c. don't waste much at all	16.9	14.3

extent to which they think public officials listen to them, they do differ somewhat in their perceptions of whether the schools are run for the benefit of all or for a few big interests. Approximately 36 percent of the compliers saw the schools as being run for a few big interests, compared to 42 percent of the avoiders. The largest differences between compliers and avoiders among the trust items occurred on waste in the public schools. Perhaps reflecting the financial hardship of paying private school tuition and school taxes, avoiders were about 10 percent more likely than compliers to think that the schools waste a lot of tax money. This also may reflect opposition to the costs imposed by busing. While these differences on the trust items are not particularly large they are consistently in the direction of less trust among avoiders.

Commitment to the Public Schools

Perhaps the most important question with regard to the characteristics of avoiders is the extent to which the loss of parents to the private schools can be expected to affect commitment to public education. In the past few years support for the public schools has become uncertain. Indeed, public willingness to support school financial referenda has declined precipitously over the past decade. Between 1960 and 1965, approximately 70 percent of all school bond issues gained majority support by the electorate. In 1972, however, only 47 percent of the bond issues presented in referenda were passed.[21] There is considerable evidence that support for school referenda is positively related to socioeconomic status. This relationship appears to arise from the greater financial ability of higher-status persons, their greater acceptance of professional judgment concerning educational needs, and the higher priority they place on education.[22]

Whether the departure of upper-status families from public schools will lead to decreased public support for educational funding is not clear from our data. When asked if it would matter much to them if the public schools closed, 90 percent of both avoiders and compliers indicated that it would. Similarly, when asked to agree or disagree with the statement, "Public schools are an important part of the American way of life," approximately 98 percent of both compliers and avoiders agreed. Clearly the long-standing importance attached by Americans to public education persists, despite desegregation or the decision to send a child to private school.

The issue of support was addressed more directly by asking respondents, "If there were a vote taken in this county on taxes to support the public schools would you vote to increase taxes, to keep taxes about the same, or to lower taxes?" The distributions for compliers and avoiders on this question were identical. Approximately 26 percent of both groups would vote to increase taxes, 59 percent to keep taxes about the same, and 15 percent to lower taxes. Of course, the extent to which actual votes will parallel these distributions is uncertain; but sending a child to private school does not appear to effect the reported willingness to support the public schools.

Support for public education, of course, is not confined to positive voting in school referenda. The schools thrive on participation of the parents in school activities. The margin between mediocrity and quality in a school is often provided by the help and time contributed voluntarily by parents, equipment purchased through their fund raising, and related activities. If avoiders are overrepresented by active parents, then the effect of their loss on the schools will be many times greater than their absolute numbers might indicate.

Respondents were asked a series of questions about their participation in school-related activities. The responses to these items are presented in table 4–4. Here there are clear-cut differences. Avoiders were drawn from parents who had provided leadership in school activities. First, while less than half of the compliers reported talking often with

Table 4–4
Participation and Avoidance

		% *Often*	% *Sometimes*	% *Seldom*	% *Never*
1. Talked to other parents to try to keep informed about school issues.	C	47.5	27.5	16.2	8.7
	A	64.1	22.7	10.1	3.1
2. Gone to meetings of the PTA, PTO, or other school organization.	C	25.9	27.9	18.7	27.4
	A	45.6	28.7	13.6	12.1
3. Gone to meetings of the school board.	C	2.7	5.8	8.1	83.4
	A	5.3	7.9	10.9	75.8
4. Worked as a teacher's aide, room mother, sports assistant, and so forth.	C	18.8	15.7	6.3	59.3
	A	30.4	21.4	7.1	41.1
5. Helped the school by raising money for school activities or by holding office in a school or educational organization.	C	23.0	24.5	8.5	43.9
	A	34.6	30.9	9.0	25.5

C = compliers; A = avoiders.

other parents about school issues, nearly two-thirds of the avoiders indicated talking often about school issues. Second, avoiders were about 20 percent more likely than compliers to indicate that they often attended meetings of PTA, PTO, or other school organizations. Third, while neither compliers nor avoiders attended school board meetings in large numbers avoiders were more likely to have attended. Finally, avoiders appear to have been the parents most often called upon or who volunteered to work in the schools and in financial drives. While a majority of the avoiders indicated that they had often or sometimes worked as teachers' aides, room mothers, and so forth, only about 35 percent of the compliers indicated a similar level of activity. Indeed, almost 60 percent of the compliers said they had never participated in any of these ways. Moreover, 65 percent of the avoiders indicated that they had often or sometimes held an office in a school organization or helped to raise funds for the school. Approximately 48 percent of the compliers gave similar responses. Thus, avoiders appear to be drawn disproportionately from among the active school parents—those who have taken a substantial interest in their children's schools and who have been willing to take on the burden of participating in school activities.

Profiles of Avoidance

For many, resistance to desegregation conjures up images of angry mobs of red-necked, bigoted southern parents aided and abetted by uniformed bullies and racist politicians. Our analysis provides a very different picture of the family that avoids desegregation by placing a child in private school. The single most prominent characteristic that distinguishes avoiders is their higher social status. Quite simply they can afford the price of private school education. Further, one of the few attitudinal variables distinguishing avoiders is class prejudice—the desire to eschew interaction with persons of lower status. Thus, the desire to avoid an interclass environment, plus the financial ability to realize it, explain why avoiders tend to be upper status.

Avoiders are virtually indistinguishable from compliers on most attitudinal dimensions. They are no more racially prejudiced than compliers, and differ little from compliers in their attitudes toward school integration, toward the legitimacy of desegregation policy, or in their sense of personal efficacy. They are more disapproving of the way school desegregation has been implemented locally, but their complaints about the desegregation process are generally the same as those given by compliers.

Even the "southernness" of resistance to desegregation is questionable. Avoiders and compliers in our districts were drawn about equally from nonsouthern migrants. Of course, migration to Florida is a largely self-selective process and the kind of individual who migrates may differ from those who do not. Consistent with nationwide surveys, however, northerners in our sample were less racially prejudiced and more tolerant toward school desegregation than southerners. The migrants, therefore, were not "closet" southerners all along.

This profile of avoidance suggests that white withdrawal, in any amount, can have important consequences for the public schools. Apart from providing alternate employment opportunities for qualified teachers and administrators, the development of private school systems in the face of desegregation also attracts another important resource away from the public schools, active and committed parents. The public schools rely on a small cadre of interested and willing parents to provide voluntary assistance in a variety of areas. When the loss of these parents is combined with the difficulty of getting any parents active in a school that may be far across town or county, the problem posed by avoidance is compounded.

The higher status character of avoiders also raises the specter of class segregation in education. Up to now, American education has not been rigidly stratified along class lines.[23] No systematic bias has existed against public school graduates because those schools have been used by the wealthier and less well-off alike. However, the disproportionate withdrawal of upper-status persons could cause the public schools to lose their place in the educational hierarchy, thus posing some problems of upward mobility for public school students.

The withdrawal of upper-status white children also reduces the possibility for interaction between lower-status blacks and middle- to upper-status whites. Such interaction was purportedly one of the beneficial conditions of desegregation for black educational achievement and for white socialization toward an integrated society.[24] This lack of an interracial experience is particularly important when one considers that the children of upper-status families have the greatest potential for providing and assuming social leadership in the future.

Upper-status persons have in the past provided a cadre of financial support for the public schools. A shift of these families to private schools could eventually weaken support for the public schools even further. Although our sample of avoiders still saw the public schools as an important social institution and were just as willing as compliers to vote taxes for the public schools, there is a question as to how long these feelings may endure. Avoiders were clearly more negative toward public school officials. In particular they were more likely to see the public schools as wasting tax dollars. These attitudes could be the leading edge to justify reduced support for school taxes. Furthermore, it must be remembered that the avoiders questioned had just placed their children in private school. Disassociation from the public schools and identification with a private school may take a few years. Indeed, it may take quite a while for the idea to sink in that the family has severed its tie to public education. So long as private school is perceived as a temporary expedient avoiders will still be concerned with supporting quality education in the public schools. Should the departure be seen as permanent, however, self-interest in the public schools will disappear, and with it, perhaps, the willingness to support them.

A few observers of school desegregation have seen a silver lining in white withdrawal. A school superintendent in one desegregating southern district asserted that white flight had not hurt his schools and added, "White flight might have been good because it got rid of all the dyed-in-wool segregationists."[25] Others have also asserted that white flight provides a "pressure valve" to release racial tensions, thereby making school desegregation easier. Our results suggest that this presumed benefit may not be realized. Since compliers are not less prejudiced than avoiders, it is hard to see how the loss of white students is thus offset by the release of racial tensions in desegregated schools.

Racism, Avoidance, and Protest: A Final Word

Some readers who have seen the demonstrations against school desegregation on television or in person and who have heard the racial epithets and slogans may doubt our findings with regard to the racial attitudes of avoiders. Two points need to be made clear. First, we are not saying that no avoiders were motivated by racial prejudice to leave desegregated public schools. Our data simply indicate that, for one reason or another, a lot of racially prejudiced people kept their children in desegregated public schools.

Second, a distinction must be made between protesting against desegregation and actually avoiding it. A little over 30 percent of the avoiders not only transferred their child to private school but also protested against school desegregation by signing petitions, attending meetings, writing to the school board, or engaging in demonstrations. On the other hand, about 20 percent of the complying parents engaged in similar behavior. An examination of these protesting parents shows them to be more racially prejudiced, more class prejudiced, and more opposed to the principle of desegregation than nonprotesters. In short, protesters come close to fitting the stereotypical image of the resister.

The majority of avoiders did not protest. They simply exercised their option to withdraw from the desegregated schools. Their names did not appear on petitions and their faces were not on television screens. On the other hand, despite their chants of "Hell no, we won't go," a lot of parents whose names did appear on petitions and whose faces were seen in demonstrations kept their children in the public schools nevertheless.

Notes

1. George E. Simpson and J. Milton Yinger, *Racial and Cultural Minorities* (New York: Harper and Row, 1965), pp. 103–108.

2. Melvin M. Tumin, *Desegregation: Resistance and Readiness* (Princeton, N.J.: Princeton University Press, 1958), p. 195.

3. See for example Robert L. Crain, *The Politics of School Desegregation* (New York: Doubleday, 1969); Thomas F. Pettigrew, "Demographic Correlates of Border-State Desegregation," *American Sociological Review,* 22 (December 1957), 683–89.

4. See for example Joshua F. Fishman, "Some Social and Psychological Determinants of Intergroups Relations in Changing Neighborhoods," *Social Forces,* 40 (October 1961), 42–51.

5. David Nevin and Robert Bills, *The Schools That Fear Built* (Washington, D.C.: Acropolis Books, 1976), pp. 71–72.

6. Charles T. Clotfelter, "School Desegregation, 'Tipping,' and Private School Enrollment," *The Journal of Human Resources* (Winter 1976), 43.

7. Nevin and Bills, *The Schools That Fear Built*, pp. 61–69.

8. Andrew M. Greeley and Paul B. Sheatsley, "Attitudes toward Racial Integration," *Scientific American,* 225 (December 1971), 13–19; *The Gallup Poll Index,* 100 (October 1973), 13–18; Melvin J. Knapp and Jon P. Alston, "White Parental Acceptance of Varying Degrees of School Desegregation: 1965 and 1970," *Public Opinion Quarterly,* 38 (Winter 1972–73), 585–91.

9. Greeley and Sheatsley, "Attitudes toward Racial Integration," 15–16.

10. Knapp and Alston, "White Parental Acceptance," 586.

11. According to the 1970 census, only 32 percent of all whites living in the state were native Floridians. U.S. Bureau of Census, *U.S. Census of Population, General Social and Economic Characteristics, 1970* (Washington, D.C.: U.S. Government Printing Office, 1972), Florida, Section 2, p. 595.

12. Jonathan Kelley, "The Politics of School Busing," *Public Opinion Quarterly* (Spring 1974), 22–39.

13. Hubert M. Blalock, "Percent Non-White and Discrimination in the South," *American Sociological Review,* 22 (December 1957), 677–82; Thomas R. Dye, "Urban School Segregation: A Comparative Analysis," *Urban Affairs Quarterly,* 2 (December 1968), 141–63; Edward E. Harris, "Prejudice and Other Social Factors in School Segregation," *Journal of Negro Education,* 37 (Fall 1968), 440–43; Thomas F. Pettigrew and M. R. Cramer, "The Demography of Desegregation," *Journal of Social Issues,* 15 (Fall 1959), 61–71; Beth E. Vanfossen, "Variables Related to Resistance to Desegregation in the South," *Social Forces,* 47 (September 1968), 39–44.

14. Tumin, *Desegregation: Resistance and Readiness,* pp. 190–93.

15. James M. Beshers, *Urban Social Structure* (New York: Free Press, 1962), pp. 128–30; Hubert M. Blalock, *Toward a Theory of Minority Group Relations* (New York: John Wiley and Sons, 1967), pp. 199–200; Edward O. Laumann, *Prestige and Association in an Urban Community* (New York: Bobbs-Merrill, 1966), p. 106; Edward O. Laumann, *Bonds of Pluralism: The Form and Substance of Urban Social Networks* (New York: John Wiley and Sons, 1973), pp. 2–8.

16. Beshers, *Urban Social Structure,* p. 128.

17. Respondents' social distance from the Smith family was ascertained using Westie's scale of residential social distance. See Frank R. Westie, "Negro-White Differentials and Social Distance," *American Sociological Review,* 17 (October 1952), 550–58; Frank R. Westie, "A

Technique for the Measurement of Race Attitudes,'' *American Sociological Review,* 18 (February 1953), 73–78; Frank R. Westie and Margaret L. Westie, ''The Social Distance Pyramid: Relations between Caste and Class,'' *American Journal of Sociology,* 63 (September 1957), 190–96.

18. Kelley, ''The Politics of School Busing,'' 26–29.

19. For a review of this literature see Charles S. Bullock and Harrell Rodgers, ''Coercion to Compliance: Southern School Districts and School Desegregation Guidelines,'' *Journal of Politics* (November 1976), 1000–1001.

20. Al Smith, Anthony Downs, and M. Leanne Lachman, *Achieving Effective Desegregation* (Lexington, Mass.: D. C. Heath Company, 1973), pp. 180–81.

21. National Center for Educational Statistics, *Bond Sales for Public School Purposes* (Washington, D.C.: U.S. Government Printing Office, 1974), p. 2.

22. James Q. Wilson and Edward C. Banfield, ''Public-Regardingness as a Value Premise in Voting Behavior,'' *American Political Science Review,* 58 (December 1964), 876–87; James A. Norton, ''Referenda Voting in a Metropolitan Area,'' *Western Political Quarterly,* 16 (March 1963), 195–212; Eugene S. Uyeki, ''Patterns of Voting in a Metropolitan Area,'' *Urban Affairs Quarterly,* 1 (June 1966), 65–77; Phillip K. Piele and John Stuart Hall, *Budgets, Bonds, and Ballots* (Lexington, Mass.: D.C. Heath, Lexington Books, 1973), pp. 114–22.

23. Charles S. Benson, ''The Transition to a New School Finance System,'' John Pincus, ed., *School Finance in Transition* (Cambridge, Mass.: Ballinger Publishing Co., 1974), p. 157.

24. Robert P. O'Reilly, *Racial and Social Class Isolation in the Schools* (New York: Praeger Publishers, 1970), chap. 3; U.S. Commission on Civil Rights, *Twenty Years After Brown: Equality of Educational Opportunity* (Washington, D.C., 1975), p. 87.

25. U.S. Commission on Civil Rights, *The Diminishing Barrier: A Report on School Desegregation in Nine Communities* (Washington, D.C., 1972), p. 46.

5 The Costs of Compliance

The decision to avoid or to comply with a public policy can be viewed in terms of the costs and benefits associated with each form of behavior.[1] If the costs of a policy outweigh its benefits, the probability of compliance with the policy decreases, *ceteris paribus*. This chapter examines the extent to which the costs of desegregation vary between avoiding and complying white parents. Two kinds of costs are examined: (1) the objective costs associated with the impact of the desegregation plan; and (2) the costs parents perceive to be associated with the plan.

School desegregation, of course, is no longer just a southern regional policy but a national issue. Despite this fact it still does not impose identical costs on all affected families. Parents are not required to comply with national desegregation guidelines, but rather with the demands of local implementation plans. And these plans, perforce, vary from district to district because school districts differ in size, percent and residential location of the black student population, the spatial arrangement of schools, the degree of racial isolation, and in a variety of other ways. Thus, even though the desegregation plans in our seven study districts were all court ordered and approved, substantial differences existed in the manner in which desegregation was implemented in each of the districts. For example, the desegregation plan for Duval County's large metropolitan district with its central city black ghetto contained features that were not necessary for implementing desegregation in the smaller, nonmetropolitan Manatee school district with its residentially scattered black population.

The impact of a court-approved plan may even vary within a particular school district. Among the seven districts, Lee County seemed to make the greatest effort to equalize the costs of its desegregation plan, yet significant cost differentials remained. While Lee County had the highest incidence of busing, a substantial minority of over 40 percent of the students still walked to a nearby school under the plan. While the county eliminated racial isolation, the proportion of black students in the schools varied nevertheless from 8 percent to 33 percent.

The costs of compliance will vary with these kinds of conditions. The objective costs clearly are lower for children who walk to a neighborhood school with a low black enrollment than for children who are bused a long distance from the neighborhood to a school with high black enrollment.

Not only may the objective costs imposed by a plan vary but parental perceptions of those costs may also vary. Parents of children assigned to the same public school may perceive that school quite differently. This variation in perception may reflect inaccuracy (for example, perceiving a predominantly white school to be predominantly black), or different standards of evaluation (for example, different views about discipline or quality in education). In either case, the perceived costs of compliance may vary even when the objective costs remain constant.

The guiding hypothesis in this chapter is that the children of avoiding parents are assessed or are perceived to be assessed higher costs to comply with desegregation than are the children of complying parents. In general, this hypothesis is examined by comparing the public schools attended by compliers' children in 1972–73 with the public schools avoiders' children were assigned to attend that year under the desegregation plan, referred to as the ''assigned public school.'' We will also refer to data on the private schools attended by the children of avoiders in 1972–73, and the public schools attended by both avoiders' and compliers' children in 1971–72. The conditions and costs associated with desegregation will be examined under four headings: (1) busing, (2) school characteristics, (3) school location, and (4) school quality, safety, and discipline.

Busing

In recent years the school desegregation controversy has centered on the use of busing to achieve racial balance. Since blacks and whites tend to live in separate neighborhoods, redrawing school attendance boundaries produces only token desegregation in many districts. To surmount this impasse, courts have required that children be assigned and bused to schools outside of their residential area.[2] The use of busing to achieve desegregation has met widespread resistance. A recent Gallup Poll showed that a majority of Americans expressed verbal approval of school desegregation, but that only 5 percent chose busing from a list of plans to achieve it.[3] In a national survey conducted for the U.S. Commission on Civil Rights, 73 percent of the white respondents said they opposed busing for school desegregation, and 58 percent said they favored a legal prohibition against it.[4] Our respondents conform to this national pattern. As was seen in the last chapter, busing was the most frequently mentioned reason for disapproving of desegregation. With the exception of Dade County, our study districts made extensive use of this unpopular implementation technique. If busing is a costly obstacle to compliance then we would certainly expect its effects to appear in our results.

Our respondents' experiences with busing are presented in table 5–1.

Table 5–1
Means of Getting to School

	% Compliers' Public Schools	*% Avoiders' Assigned Public Schools*	*% Avoiders' Private Schools*
School Bus	50.3	53.9	37.7
Car Pool	27.2	20.1	49.5
Walk-Bike	17.9	22.3	8.7
Other	4.6	3.7	4.3

Surprisingly, avoiders were not heavily drawn from the families whose children experienced busing. Their children were only slightly more likely (3 percent) than compliers' to have ridden a bus to the assigned public school. Furthermore, the avoidance decision increased the probability that the child would have to be transported to school. Slightly more than 87 percent of the avoiders said that their child either rode a bus or traveled in a car pool to private school. By contrast, 74 percent would have reached their assigned public school by similar means. Thus, the cost of transportation appears to be one that avoiders are more than willing to bear to send a child to private school.

Opposition to busing, of course, does not simply focus on the form of transportation. Much of the protest has centered on the fact that children are not attending their local, neighborhood school and the accompanying fact that they have to travel longer distances to school. The following responses were typical:

Respondent #850289:
I don't think it is fair to bus children from one end of town to the other. . . . I think a child spending too much time on a bus is bad.

Respondent #973002:
. . . Each child should go to the neighborhood school to spend more time studying instead of traveling on buses.

In table 5–2, the distance compliers' children traveled one way to public school is compared with two distance figures for avoiders' children: (1) the distance one way to the assigned public school; and (2) the distance one way to private school. As can be seen, the distances were virtually identical between the public school for compliers and the assigned public schools for avoiders, showing clearly that avoiders' children were not scheduled for longer bus rides under the desegregation plan. Moreover, for avoiders' children, their private school was much less likely to fall within a two-mile radius of home than their assigned public school. On average, then, the children of avoiders traveled greater dis-

Table 5–2
Distance to School

Miles	*% Compliers' Public Schools*	*% Avoiders' Assigned Public Schools*	*% Avoiders' Private Schools*
0–2	49.9	46.0	31.6
3–5	21.6	21.9	30.7
6–8	9.8	9.0	15.8
9–11	5.3	6.2	9.1
12+	13.4	16.9	12.8

tances to attend private school than they would have to attend public school.

The experience with busing apparently has little if any influence on avoidance. Compliers' children were just as likely as avoiders' to be bused to public school, and over comparable distances. In addition, the children of avoiders were actually more likely to be transported and to travel greater distances to private school than would have been the case had they gone to the assigned public school.

The limited influence of busing is confirmed by examining the explanations avoiders gave for placing a child in private school. Only about 13 percent of the avoiders cited busing as the most important reason for sending a child to private school, and even among them the causal linkage between busing and avoidance is problematic. For example, respondent #150201 justified placing his child in private school by stating, "She was to go to [name of school] which meant she'd ride a bus when she could have walked to [name of public school.]." This same child was bused five miles to private school. Thus, while verbally objecting to busing to a desegregated public school, this respondent simultaneously accepted busing to a segregated private school.

Earlier we saw that approximately 30 percent of both avoiders and compliers cited busing as a reason for disapproving of desegregation. How does this square with the apparent lack of an empirical relationship between an actual experience with busing and avoidance? The main reason for this disparity is that many respondents simply disapproved of busing in the abstract. Respondents whose children were not assigned to a bus ride were just as likely to cite busing as a reason for disapproval as were parents whose children were assigned to ride a bus. Thus, verbal opposition to busing was not associated with having actually experienced it. Accordingly, verbal disapproval of busing provides little basis for predicting avoidance. Apparently busing is not a source of avoidance, but rather a symbol whites use to justify their disapproval of desegregation.

School Characteristics

Percent Black Enrollment

Desegregation policymakers commonly assume that the decision to withdraw a child from a desegregated school is conditioned by the percent black student enrollment. For example, the federal district court in *U.S.* v. *Board of School Commissioners, Indianapolis, Indiana* concluded that "when the percent of black pupils . . . approaches 40 more or less the white exodus becomes accelerated and irreversible."[5] Similarly, in the Wilmington, Delaware, desegregation case the court justified the inclusion of the predominantly white Newark school district in the desegregation plan by asserting that "the stability of any desegregation plan is enhanced by the inclusion of . . . higher white concentrations."[6]

The hypothesis linking percent black enrollment and white withdrawal is supported by three bodies of evidence. First, several studies have found a positive relationship between the percent black enrollment in a district and the rate at which school desegregation occurs.[7] Indeed, Robey, in an examination of segregation in 872 southern county school districts in 1968, determined that "the single strongest explanatory variable [was] the percent of the population Negro in 1960."[8]

Second, attitudinal research has shown that verbal opposition to desegregation increases with higher black ratios in the schools. Analyzing a national survey of white attitudes toward school desegregation, Knapp and Alston found that 30 percent of the southern respondents and 21 percent of the northern respondents would object to desegregation if blacks formed half of the student body, but that an additional 27 percent of the southerners and 31 percent of the northerners would object if blacks were more than half.[9]

Third, several recent studies have found that declines in white student enrollments in desegregated school districts increase with the level of black concentration.[10] Some studies have found a threshold in the black/white ratio below which whites are insensitive to variations in the black concentration but above which withdrawal occurs. For example, a study of enrollment stability in 100 desegregated southern school systems found that over a two-year period districts with less than 35 percent black enrollments on average experienced no declines in white student enrollment. By contrast, districts above 35 percent black experienced losses and their size increased with the percent black enrollment.[11] Other studies have found white withdrawal to increase with the level of black enrollment without any threshold effect. In their Baltimore study, Arthur Stinchcombe and others concluded that "there is no 'tipping point.' Or rather, the 'tipping point' is zero. . . . Once a school is desegregated . . . the

Table 5–3
Percent Black School Enrollments

	% Compliers' Public Schools	*% Avoiders' Assigned Public Schools*
0–10	15.2	12.3
11–20	24.6	16.8
21–30	21.5	18.9
31–40	13.6	22.6
41–50	12.4	19.0
51–60	2.9	8.0
61–70	0.8	0.5
71–80	8.2	1.5
81–90	0.1	0.7
90–100	—	—

proportion Negro is likely to go up each year in a steady fashion. . . ."[12] Thus, while the structure of the relationship between percent black enrollment and white withdrawal is debatable, its existence is uncontested.

Racial balances in the public schools varied considerably both between our study districts and within them. Using official school district records for all the public schools, table 5–3 shows the distributions by percent black enrollment for compliers' public schools and for avoiders' assigned public schools. These data show that the children of avoiders were assigned, on average, to schools with higher black concentrations. Over 60 percent of the compliers' children, but only 48 percent of the avoiders' children, were assigned to attend schools 30 percent black or less. Avoiders' children were also considerably more likely to be assigned to schools between one-third and one-half black. They were not, however, disproportionately assigned to majority black schools.

The cost associated with a given level of black concentration may vary with previous experience. For example, assignment to a school 45 percent black poses less change and hence lower cost for a child who attended a school 35 percent black the previous year than for a child who attended a school 10 percent black. On average, avoiders experienced a larger change than compliers in the black enrollments in their children's schools. For compliers the black enrollments in the 1972–73 schools averaged 2.6 percent higher than the previous year. For avoiders the black enrollment in the assigned public school was more than 9 percent higher on average than in the previous year's public school. Viewed somewhat differently, about one-third of the compliers' children who were assigned to attend schools above 30 percent black in 1972–73 had attended schools less than 30 percent black the year before. The comparable figure for avoiders' children was approximately 60 percent. Thus, not only were the children of avoiders assigned to schools with higher black enrollments, but they also would have experienced larger increases in black enrollment than the children of compliers.

Are parents aware of the precise racial balances in the schools? The systematic effects of the percent black variable suggest that they are. Prior research, however, has shown that whites tend to perceive a greater black presence in their environment than actually exists.[13] Parental perceptions of the racial composition of the schools were ascertained by asking compliers to estimate the black enrollment in the schools their children attended, and avoiders to estimate the black enrollment in the public schools their children would have attended. About 60 percent of the respondents were able to give exact percentages. Within this subsample, 65 percent overestimated the black enrollment by more than 10 percent; 25 percent were able to place the black enrollment within 10 percent of its actual figure; the remaining 10 percent of the respondents underestimated. While the estimates were on the high side, they did tend to increase with the actual black enrollment. That is, parents with children assigned to attend schools that were 20 percent black tended to give lower estimates of black enrollment than parents whose children were assigned to schools 30 or 40 percent black. Moreover, the distributions of estimated black percentages in the schools were virtually identical for both compliers and avoiders. Thus, while our respondents' estimates were imprecise, they were nevertheless sensitive to the racial balances in the schools.

Previous Status of the School

School officials in desegregating districts often fear that white parents will be especially resistant to sending their children to formerly black schools. Paint-up/fix-up campaigns for black schools are frequently part of a desegregation plan, and school officials often will change the names of formerly black schools to remove the "stigma" of their segregated past.

On the basis of school district records, all the public schools in the seven districts were classified according to their racial status prior to desegregation. As can be seen in table 5–4, while avoiders' children were

Table 5–4
Previous Status of the Public School

	% Compliers' Public Schools	*% Avoiders' Assigned Public Schools*
Black	20.3	28.5
White	55.3	53.9
Integrated	24.1	17.6

about 8 percent more likely to be assigned to formerly black schools, the vast majority of children were assigned to schools that were white or already desegregated to some extent. Parental perceptions of a school's prior status were very accurate. Less than two percent misclassified a formerly black school as white.

Condition of the School

The attempt to rehabilitate formerly black schools tends to validate frequent complaints by black parents that the condition of their schools is ignored by white school administrations. It also shows that those same administrators believe that white parents base their compliance/avoidance decisions in part of the physical condition of the assigned public school. By mail questionnaire, school officials were asked to evaluate the physical condition of all the public schools in their districts. As might be expected, nearly all the schools were rated as being in good condition. While the children of avoiders were 5 percent less likely to be assigned to schools in "good" condition, over 90 percent of all the children were assigned to schools rated in that category. Thus, the overwhelming majority of avoiders chose not to send their children to public schools which were considered by school authorities to be in good shape.

Of course, the way parents view the condition of the schools may be more important than the ratings of school officials. While our respondents were less willing than school authorities to make favorable evaluations, large majorities of both groups (76 percent for compliers; 71 percent for avoiders) rated their children's assigned schools as being in good condition. Thus, seven out of every ten avoiders refused to send their children to public schools they themselves felt were in good shape.

The status of a school prior to desegregation influenced parental evaluations of its conditions. Among parents whose children were assigned to a formerly white or integrated school, over 75 percent evaluated the physical condition as good. When the assigned school was formerly black, only 55 percent gave favorable evaluations, which may, in fact, accurately reflect the condition of those schools prior to the implementation of desegregation.

Percent Black in the Neighborhood

Studies of residential segregation and housing choice indicate that the racial concentration in a neighborhood is a central characteristic used by whites to evaluate its attractiveness. Whites tend to leave neighborhoods as blacks move in, and white demand for houses in an area tends to decline with black inmigration.[14] The racial characteristics of the area surrounding a school may serve as an indicator to white parents of the general neighborhood environment, and assignment to a school in a predominantly black neighborhood may be viewed as costly by white parents. As one of our respondents (#150143) stated, "I didn't like the public school that Mike was assigned to. It is in a black area and I felt that he wouldn't be safe there."

The racial characteristics of the areas surrounding the assigned public schools were measured by U.S. Census figures for racial balances in the specific tracts in which the schools were located and all contiguous tracts. The distribution of school assignments by percent black in the area is presented in table 5–5. Avoiders' children were slightly more likely than compliers' to be assigned to schools in predominantly black neighborhoods. Approximately 17 percent of the compliers' children attended public schools in areas 90 percent or more black while 24 percent of the avoiders' children were assigned to schools in such areas. However, about 60 percent of the children from both respondent groups were assigned to attend schools in areas 20 percent black or less. Thus, while avoiders were more likely than compliers to be assigned to schools in black areas, the majority of avoiders in fact refused to send their children to schools in predominantly white neighborhoods.

The actual racial balance in the area surrounding a school, again, may be less important than what the respondents perceive the racial composition to be. Compliers' estimates were very close to the objective census measure. About 25 percent said the school areas were predominantly black, while 59 percent said they were all or mostly all white. By contrast

Table 5–5
Racial Mix of Area

% Black	*% Compliers' Public Schools*	*% Avoiders' Assigned Public Schools*
0	39.9	47.6
1–10	20.9	11.6
11–20	3.8	2.5
21–30	3.4	1.3
31–40	2.2	6.1
41–50	.2	.3
51–60	.9	.9
61–70	9.8	.3
71–80	.8	4.0
81–90	1.3	1.2
91–100	17.2	24.0

57 percent of the avoiders thought the public schools their children were assigned to attend were located in predominantly black areas. Thus, while a majority of avoiders' children were actually assigned to attend public schools in predominantly white areas, a majority thought their children were assigned to schools in predominantly black areas, and therefore perceived a far higher cost for compliance than was actually imposed.

Condition of the Area

Respondent #250435 explained her avoidance this way:

After seeing the school, I could not subject Elissa Anne to that. I made many trips over there at recess time to see what's going on. The neighborhood was run down, it just was terrible. . . . The neighborhood is just real run down, she'd see that day after day after day and eventually she'd get to where she'd hate to go to school. . . .

At least in some districts parental concern about the condition of the neighborhoods in which schools are located is shared by school officials and federal district judges. In Duval County, for example, at least three schools were closed under the desegregation plan because of their location in deteriorated, crime-ridden areas. (Parenthetically, we should observe that these schools were safe enough to operate so long as they served only black students.)

Planning and engineering officials in the counties were asked by mail questionnaire to estimate the condition of the areas surrounding the public schools. The results are not in the expected direction. Approximately 45 percent of the avoiders' children and 39 percent of the compliers' children were assigned to public schools located in areas evaluated as well kept; 15 percent of the avoiders' children and 18 percent of the compliers' children were assigned to public schools in areas evaluated as run down. Majorities of both compliers and avoiders evaluated the areas surrounding the assigned public schools as being well kept and avoiders were only slightly more likely than compliers to evaluate the areas as run down.

Census data tend to confirm the minimal differences in areas surrounding the assigned public schools. The median property value in the census tracts of assigned schools was $13,450 for compliers and $13,799 for avoiders. However, the median property value of the census tract for the assigned public school in the previous year was $15,200 for avoiders and $13,800 for compliers. Either by objective measures or subjective estimates of officials or respondents, the condition of the areas surrounding the assigned public schools for 1972–73 differed little between avoiders and compliers. Avoiders' children, however, attended public schools in better areas the previous year and thus experienced a greater change from one year to the next. Thus, the condition of the area surrounding the school seems to bear on avoidance only marginally when a child is reassigned from an area higher in property value to one lower.

School Quality

The available evidence suggests that desegregation does not materially affect one way or the other the academic achievement of white children and, therefore, the quality of their education.[15] Their parents, however, may have a hard time accepting that fact. Desegregation does change the learning environment for a child, and it is a fact that some parents wonder about the effects of having culturally deprived students in their own children's classrooms and the alteration of the school curriculum to meet the needs of a biracial, multi-class school population. Assessing the quality of a school is, of course, a highly subjective matter. Accreditation might be a useful guide, but few parents are aware of accreditation procedures or even whether their child's school has received state or regional accreditation. Thus much depends on the eye of the beholder, and people often see things differently. Some may see the introduction of vocational programs in a school's curriculum as compromising quality; others will note that the school still offers advanced mathematics and science and not be disturbed. Some may view the presence of minority students as reducing the time and attention their own children can expect to receive in class; others will reassure themselves that the teachers are equally interested in all the students and will relate to them accordingly.

Because these kinds of judgments are highly subjective it may be questioned whether they produce a particular behavior or are the product of that behavior. For example, avoiders might be more negative than compliers in their evaluations of public school quality in justification of their decision to leave. Or avoiders might evaluate their new private schools favorably in justification of the financial costs incurred by sending the children there. However, an assessment of our respondents' perceptions should indicate a good deal about public views of school quality in the aftermath of desegregation. In addition, while the perceptions of avoiders may be predictable, those of compliers are not; and it is hardly immaterial to inquire whether the consumers of desegregated public education are satisfied with the product.

The most commonly mentioned reason for sending a child to private school was the quality of education. Over 40 percent of the avoiders believed that a private school education was superior to a public school education. Accordingly, 70 percent of the avoiders were highly satisfied with the quality of courses and instruction in their children's private schools. By contrast, about 58 percent of the avoiders were satisfied with the education their children received in public school the year before, and close to half of them (44 percent) felt the education was below average in the public schools their children would have attended under the desegregation plan.

Compliers were much more likely to evaluate the quality of public education favorably. Approximately 80 percent of them were at least satisfied with the quality of education in the previous year's public schools. However, compared to the large majority of avoiders who were highly satisfied with private school education, only 30 percent of the compliers were highly satisfied with the education their children were receiving in their public schools for the current year. These differences appear traceable in part to different perceptions about academic standards in the schools. When asked why they were so satisfied with private school education, about 12 percent of the avoiders said it was because the private schools were demanding scholastically. Only about 3 percent of the compliers said that high academic standards were the reason for their satisfaction with the public schools. If these relative assessments are not precisely true, they are at least consistent. When asked if there was anything they didn't like about their children's schools, compliers were far more likely than avoiders to say that the level of instruction was too easy, and while some avoiders felt that private school education might be even too demanding, almost none of the compliers said that about the public schools.

Avoiders also typically mentioned smaller classes and greater individualized attention as reasons for choosing private schools and being satisfied with them.

Respondent #450046:
He was not getting enough individual attention and the classrooms were too large. The pupil/teacher ratio was too high.

Respondent #550021:
Better tutoring and more attention in private school.

While 20 percent of the avoiders cited small classes and more attention from the teacher as reasons for their satisfaction with private schools, only about 3 percent of the compliers mentioned these reasons as the basis for their satisfaction with the public schools. Of course, this could mean that compliers simply have different priorities. It is significant, however, that even some of the satisfied compliers complained that their children's classes were too large and that their children consequently were not receiving enough personal attention. Thus, whether real or imagined, both compliers and avoiders shared the belief that the public schools were understaffed.

While avoiders perceived the public schools less favorably than compliers, the fact remains that they kept their children in the public schools until they became desegregated. One might assume that complaints about quality are simply a front for racial hostility, except for the fact that we saw in Chapter 4 that avoiders were not any more racially prejudiced than compliers. How, then, are desegregation, perceptions of quality, and avoidance linked together? Earlier it was shown that avoiders' children were somewhat more likely than compliers' to be assigned to formerly black schools. They were also more likely to believe that the quality of education was below average when the assigned school was formerly black (over 50 percent) than when it was white (about 40 percent). Thus the combination of assessed and perceived costs conveyed to avoiders the possibility that desegregated education could result in inferior education.

Perhaps because of this avoiders were also somewhat more likely than compliers to believe that desegregation was harmful to white students. Respondents were given the statement: "White students' test scores have fallen sharply in integrated schools." The statement is false, but a majority of all respondents thought it was true. Avoiders, however, were even more likely than compliers to think so (72 percent versus 64 percent).

What impact does desegregation have on parents' views about the quality of public education? Parents who leave the public schools obviously feel that the costs of avoidance are repaid by an education of higher quality for their children. They believe the quality of public education to be lower, and they do attribute the qualitative difference, in part, to desegregation of the public schools. Parents who remain with the public schools seem relatively satisfied with their quality. However, they are less satisfied with the public schools than avoiders are with the private schools. The benefits of private schooling are particularly appealing for parents who desire a demanding academic environment for their children. Not even satisfied compliers thought that public school academic standards were particularly demanding.

Both groups of parents shared some concerns about staff size and attention for students in the public schools. But whereas some parents felt those problems were serious enough to choose the private school alternative, others apparently did not.

Lest we conclude that avoiders and compliers beheld differences in the quality of public education simply because they made different decisions about the schooling of their children, one final point should be made. Whether they left their children in public schools or pulled them out, a sizable majority of all white parents actually believed that desegregation would adversely affect their children's academic achievement, at least as measured by standardized test scores.

Discipline and Safety

Next to educational quality, parents feel that a disciplined, safe learning environment is the most important characteristic for a school. In fact, most parents feel that discipline is an essential component of quality education. Some typical responses from our parents were:

Respondent #150146:
He wasn't learning. There was a lack of discipline in the classroom.

Respondent #150147:
I think he can get a better education in Tallahassee Christian. They're more strict and in public school they don't care whether they know anything or not.

Respondent #850491:
I feel that there are a lower class of blacks in the school. I feel that we are upper middle class and this creates conflict.

There was widespread dissatisfaction with discipline in the public schools among all parents in the seven counties. Almost 40 percent of the compliers said that discipline was a problem in the public schools their children were attending, and over 50 percent of the avoiders said the same thing about the public schools their children had attended the year before. Moreover, about 75 percent of the avoiders thought discipline was a problem in the assigned public schools from which they withdrew their children.

These sentiments were not just the product of idle speculation. Forty-five percent of the compliers reported that their children had experienced problems in their public schools, almost all of which involved theft or some kind of physical violence directed toward their children. A majority of compliers said these incidents occurred more than once. Almost half of the avoiders (44 percent) indicated that their children had experienced similar problems in public school the year before.

While we had no way to check the veracity of each of these reports, school officials acknowledged that these kinds of incidents did occur in their schools from time to time; special security forces or teams of parents patrolled the corridors and restrooms in some particularly tense schools; occasionally a school in one or another of the districts would be closed following a serious clash between white and black students; and in one county, two schools (a middle school and a high school) received bomb threats repeatedly. Therefore, parental fears were not idle, and the exposure of children to a potentially threatening physical environment would certainly be a cost all parents could attach to compliance.

The Potential of Avoidance

Perhaps the most striking conclusion to be drawn from the materials in this chapter is that so many white parents comply with school desegregation despite relatively high objective and perceived costs. Even with a high incidence of busing, assignment of children to formerly black schools, concerns about educational quality, and fears about safety and discipline within the schools, many white parents, indeed most of them, continue to send their children to the public schools. Does this mean that the difference between compliers and avoiders reduces itself to the fact that compliers are indifferent to the costs of desegregation, or that they are steadfastly loyal to the public schools despite those costs? Our data suggest otherwise. About 30 percent of our compliers indicated that they had considered sending their children to private school. Comparing these potential avoiders to the rest of the compliers, it was found that they perceived or were assessed higher costs to comply. Their children were about 15 percent more likely to be bused to school, 18 percent less likely to live within five miles of their public school, 13 percent more likely to attend formerly black schools, and 13 percent more likely to attend schools with higher black enrollments (over 30 percent). Potential avoiders were also considerably less satisfied than the other compliers with the quality of instruction in the public schools, and almost twice as likely to indicate that discipline and safety were problems in their children's public schools. Thus in terms of the costs of compliance, the potential avoiders resembled very closely the actual avoiders.

What explains the gap between the potential for avoidance and its actual occurrence? The answer, pure and simple, is financial. Two-thirds of the potential avoiders cited the prohibitive costs of private school tuition as the main reason for keeping their children in the public schools. Thus the decision to avoid can be conceptualized as a two-step process involving first the predisposition to avoid and, second, the means to avoid. Consideration of the private school alternative is conditioned by the costs of compliance, those objectively imposed by the features of the desegregation plan, and those that parents subjectively perceive. As the costs of compliance increase, the probability of considering avoidance also increases. This potential for avoidance, however, is not translated directly and uniformly into the corresponding behavior because the "cost calculus" employed by parents is not one of weighing the costs of desegregation against its benefits, but rather one of weighing the costs of compliance against the costs of avoidance. The costs of compliance may predispose parents to avoid, but for most of them the costs of avoidance make it necessary to comply. Since the costs of avoidance are primarily financial (tuition and transportation) the threshold for crossing from compliance to avoidance is high and negotiable only for those with sufficient family income. Thus, when flight from desegregated schools is low, it is not necessarily because the potential for withdrawal is not there, but rather because the means to withdraw is limited to a relatively small segment of the population.

The Policymaker's Costs

What are some of the implications of our findings for desegregation policy planning? How should policymakers themselves assess the costs of implementing desegregation? It would seem that busing and assignment of white students to formerly black schools to eliminate racial isolation can be employed extensively without necessarily resulting in widespread withdrawal from the public schools. To be sure, desegregation produces some avoidance and these implementation techniques invite a considerable potential for more. However, that potential seems to go largely unrealized. The advantage for desegregation policy planners is that for most parents the costs of compliance are exceeded by the costs of avoidance. While a little less busing, shorter busing distances, and the conversion of formerly black schools to other than classroom use might reduce avoidance a little, that marginal benefit could be neutralized by placing a heavier burden for desegregation on blacks, or by producing a greater degree of racial imbalance in some schools which might, in turn, invite a little more avoidance than would occur otherwise. The most effective approach to desegregation planning, therefore, would seem to be to employ whatever reasonable implementation techniques are available to equalize the costs of compliance among all affected families. Currying the favor of possible avoiders would seem to be a losing proposition anyway; recall that many if not most of the avoiders sent their children to private school even though the desegregation plan assigned them to a nearby, formerly white school.

Far more than the physical techniques of desegregation, policymakers need to be concerned with the academic image of their desegregated schools. For avoiders, the main appeal of private academies was the belief that they sustained a level of educational quality that was being eroded in the public schools by desegregation. Furthermore, they were willing to transport their children more often and over longer distances for the perceived qualitative benefits than would have been the case had they kept their children in the public schools. Some of the compliers as well were dissatisfied with quality, safety, and discipline in the public schools. Apparently few of them equated public education with high academic standards, and most felt that desegregation impaired academic achievement. Thus dissatisfaction and avoidance will continue to be problems until school officials can communicate effectively to parents that, while a desegregated educational experience differs from a segregated one, it does not necessarily follow that it is inferior.

Notes

1. Anthony Downs, *An Economic Theory of Democracy* (New York: Harper & Row, 1957); Robert B. Stover and Don W. Brown, "Understanding Compliance and Non-Compliance with Law: The Contribution of Utility Theory," *Social Science Quarterly,* 56 (December 1975), 363–75; Harrell Rodgers, Jr., and Charles S. Bullock, III, *Law and Social Change: Civil Rights Laws and Their Consequences* (New York: McGraw-Hill, 1972), pp. 181–209.
2. *Swann* v. *Charlotte-Mecklenberg,* 402 U.S. 1, 1971.
3. *Gallup Poll,* 100th Issue, p. 18.
4. Marvin Wall, "What the Public Doesn't Know," *Civil Rights Digest,* 5 (Summer 1973), 23–27.
5. 322 F. Supp. 655.
6. *Evans* v. *Buchanan,* 379 F. Supp. 1218 (D. Del. 1974).
7. Thomas Dye, "Urban School Segregation: A Comparative Analysis," *Urban Affairs Quarterly,* 2 (December 1968), 141–63; Edward Harris, "Prejudice and Other Social Factors in School Segregation," *Journal of Negro Education,* 37 (Fall 1968), 440–43; Thomas Pettigrew, "Demographic Correlates of Border State Desegregation," *American Sociological Review,* 22 (December 1957), 683–89.
8. John Robey, "The Politics of School Desegregation: A Policy Analysis of Policy Outcome in Southern Counties," Ph.D. Thesis, University of Georgia, 1970.
9. Melvin J. Knapp and Jon Alston, "White Parental Acceptance of Varying Degrees of School Desegregation," *Public Opinion Quarterly,* 36 (Winter 1972–73), 585–91.
10. Charles Clotfelter, "School Desegregation, 'Tipping,' and Private School Enrollment," *Journal of Human Resources,* 11 (Winter 1976), 28–49; Luther Munford, "White Flight from Desegregation in Mississippi," *Integrated Education,* 11 (May-June 1973), 12–26.
11. Micheal W. Giles, "School Desegregation and White With-

drawal: A Test of the Tipping-Point Model,'' Florida Atlantic University, mimeo, 1977.

12. Arthur Stinchcombe, Mary McDill, and Dollie Walker, ''Is There a Racial Tipping Point in Changing Schools?'' *Journal of Social Issues,* 25 (November 1, 1969), 127–36.

13. Sidney Hollander and Lorraine Scarpa, ''A Note on the Perception of Race,'' *Public Opinion Quarterly* (Winter 1971–72), 606–607.

14. James S. Miller, ''Factors Affecting Racial Mixing in Residential Areas,'' in Amos H. Hawley and Vincent Roch, *Segregation in Residential Areas* (Washington, D.C., National Academy of Science, 1973), pp. 148–71.

15. Nancy St. John, *School Desegregation: Outcomes for Children* (New York: John Wiley and Sons, 1975).

6 Black and White Parental Support for School Desegregation: Some Similarities and Differences

In addition to the problem of minimizing flight to the private schools and maintaining stable racial balances in the public schools, educational policymakers face yet another problem that relates to attitudinal support of parents for desegregation. The fact that most parents of school children have complied behaviorally with desegregation does not necessarily signify their approval of it either in principle or in practice. To the extent that parents have negative views of desegregated schooling a residue of important problems remains for school policymakers.

Behavioral compliance aside, parents' attitudinal support or nonsupport for desegregation may have significant policy consequences. For example, the authors have previously reported that white compliers having unfavorable views of local implementation plans are generally unwilling to lend personal assistance to school activities or to vote in favor of school funding in referenda; contrastingly, compliers who view local implementation favorably tend to be willing to aid their school systems in both respects.[1] Nancy St. John has reviewed several studies suggesting that parents' hostility to desegregation may often "rub off" on their children and negatively affect their behavior in school.[2] Community hostility to desegregation often triggers interracial violence and other forms of deviant behavior in the schools, and leads to political pressures upon public officials at all levels to modify or restrict desegregation planning. In short, grudging compliance is hardly a firm foundation for building racial harmony in a benign and constructive educational environment. What is at stake is not only the minimization of resegregation but also the maximization of community attitudinal support for racially unitary school systems.

Hostility toward school desegregation has stemmed primarily from white parents and their social and political leaders. Blacks in a few communities founded alternative schools in the late 1960s and early 1970s, but on the whole, black Americans appear to have welcomed desegregation as the harbinger of a new equality and expanded educational opportunities for their children. However, while black support for desegregation in principle appears high, their support for it in practice cannot be taken for granted. National polls have indicated that many blacks share white misgivings about busing for the purpose of desegregation.[3] In some desegregated schools, black children have faced verbal abuse or outright violence from whites, and they may also sense prejudicial treatment from white teachers. Hence, while school desegregation may promise a brighter future for black children, its present costs to them may sometimes be high.

Of course, any disillusionment among blacks with desegregation in practice will rarely be expressed in flight from the public to private schools because the financial burden of a private school education is too heavy for most black parents to bear. Out of a total of 1,434 private school avoiders in our seven-county study, only 48 (3.3 percent) were black. Underlying uniform behavioral compliance among blacks, however, there may be reactions against the costs imposed on black children by local desegregation plans, and perhaps a measure of opposition to school desegregation *per se*. Nonsupport among black parents can also be expected to have the same policy ramifications as among whites. Even though blacks are a minority in most American school districts, their attitudinal support is likely to be of critical importance for the long-run success of school desegregation as a public policy.

In this chapter, then, we will present comparisons in support for desegregation among black and white parents in our sample. We shall begin with responses to a question eliciting summary evaluations of desegregation as implemented in the seven school districts. We shall then attempt to discover some major factors that shape parental support. Are parental views of local implementation influenced by factors over which policymakers have some degree of control—for example, the impacts of desegregation plan features on children? Or, are parental opinions of desegregation in practice largely determined by basic, longer-range predispositions—for example, white prejudice, black separatism—that policymakers can do little to change at least in the short run? What, if anything, might school policymakers do to increase public attitudinal support for desegregation in their local districts?

Parental Views of Desegregation in Practice

Table 6–1 reports parental responses to the question, "In general, how do you feel about the way desegregation has been handled around here?" The distribution of responses across five precoded categories is significantly different for white and black compliers. As the table shows, approximately 60 percent of the whites either "disapprove" or "disapprove strongly" of desegregation in practice in their districts. Less than 25 percent of the white compliers held favorable views, while the rest were ambivalent.

Table 6–1
"In General, How Do You Feel About the Way Desegregation Has Been Handled around Here?"

	% White Parents	*% Black Parents*
Approve strongly	2.2	9.3
Approve	21.6	46.3
Neither approve nor disapprove	15.8	17.7
Disapprove	29.9	18.4
Disapprove strongly	30.0	8.0
Don't know; not sure	.2	.3

The distribution of black responses runs in the opposite direction. A majority of about 55 percent had positive opinions. About one-fourth of the black compliers had negative views, while the remainder said they neither approved nor disapproved. Clearly, then, widespread behavioral compliance cannot be taken as an indicator of subjective support. Out of our total sample of compliers, only about one-third said that they approved of the handling of desegregation in their school districts.

Attitudes toward Desegregation in Principle

Views of desegregation in practice may be influenced, in part, by root attitudes concerning race relations. For example, white prejudices against blacks are often ingrained in childhood and are not easily changed in adult life. Hence, prejudiced whites may take a dim view of any measures to desegregate the public schools even if their children experience no direct impacts from the local implementation plan. Similarly, perhaps some black parents disapprove of the local handling of desegregation not from their objections to busing or other plan impacts but from a deeper concern for maintaining black identity and social cohesion. Conversely, parents of both races who are committed to integration as an ideal may applaud the local implementation plan even if it imposes heavy demands on them and their children.

Several of our interview items, reported in table 6–2, were designed to tap basic attitudes toward biracial schooling as a broad social goal. These data show that whites tend to be more supportive of desegregation in principle than in practice. Majorities of our white respondents felt that schools ought to be desegregated to promote interracial understanding, and agreed with the prediction that desegregated schools would bring about more harmonious race relations in the future. A near majority of whites agreed that school desegregation would give black children the

Table 6–2
Basic Attitudes Concerning School Desegregation

I. *Attitudes toward school integration in principle:*

"Schools ought to be integrated to help black and white children understand each other better."

	% Agree	% Neither	% Disagree
Whites	56.7	2.9	40.4
Blacks	91.8	2.1	6.1

"Different races will get along better someday if they all go to school together now."

	% Agree	% Neither	% Disagree
Whites	66.1	3.6	30.3
Blacks	94.1	1.9	4.0

"School integration will help give black children the rights they should have had all along."

	% Agree	% Neither	% Disagree
Whites	46.4	3.5	50.1
Blacks	94.1	1.7	4.2

II. *Attitudes toward the legitimacy of government actions:*

"The government has no right to tell you where to send your child to school."

	% Agree	% Neither	% Disagree
Whites	83.7	1.6	14.8
Blacks	47.5	5.2	47.3

"The Supreme Court doesn't have any business making decisions about school integration."

	% Agree	% Neither	% Disagree
Whites	62.4	3.9	33.7
Blacks	27.4	8.0	64.7

"No matter what local school officials think, they should do what the courts say about school integration."

	% Agree	% Neither	% Disagree
Whites	49.6	5.8	44.5
Blacks	80.1	4.0	15.9

rights to which they were entitled. Not surprisingly, responses of whites to these items were closely related to their replies to other items in our survey measuring prejudice against black people. The stereotype of white southerners as racially prejudiced contains no small element of truth; yet at the same time roughly half of the white respondents appeared sympathetic to desegregation as a matter of principle.

Moreover, there appears only a mere trace of evidence of separatist attitudes among blacks. As table 6–2 shows, over 90 percent of the black parents felt that school desegregation would give black children their rights and also further interracial understanding. Almost uniformly, black parents saw biracial schooling as an avenue to a better future life for their children. In short, black enthusiasm for biracial education in principle appears virtually unanimous.

Further, support for school desegregation as a general ideal appears to be an important influence on approval of local desegregation in practice, particularly among white parents. For white compliers, the simple correlation between support for desegregation in principle and in practice is .503. From a coefficient of this magnitude, we can infer that basic predispositions of whites toward biracial schooling have a fairly strong impact on their approval of desegregation practices in their districts.

For black parents, the statistical relationship between these two variables approaches zero (r = .084). However, the weakness of this coefficient is almost surely a statistical peculiarity rather than a meaningful indicator of the impact of black attitudes toward school desegregation or support of it locally. For, as we have seen, black parents agree virtually unanimously with the idea of school desegregation. Therefore, it is unsafe to infer that basic attitudes of blacks toward school desegregation in principle fail to affect their support for desegregation in practice. Perhaps the safer assumption is that, for blacks as well as for whites, a basic commitment to the ideal of school desegregation is a strong foundation of support for local desegregation practices.

Attitudes toward the Legitimacy of Governmental Action

Approval of school desegregation as a matter of principle may not signify a belief that government has a moral right to mandate desegregation. In the course of our interviews, many white parents said that they believed in the integration of the schools but that it was being "pushed too fast," or that it should come about by "majority rule" rather than by judicial decisions or other forms of governmental intervention. It is difficult to interpret statements of this sort. At times, they may be no more than thinly veiled hypocrisy. Views of this kind may also arise out of a populistic ideology that sees any policymaking by government as justified only through mass consultation and consent, and that looks upon decision-making by courts and bureaucracies as a violation of democratic procedures. Moreover, the widespread feeling that government has no right to intervene in local school affairs may be reinforced by the well-documented decline in Americans' faith in their established governmental institutions.[4] For whatever reasons, rejection of the legitimacy of governmental action to desegregate the schools may be an important determinant of disapproval of local implementation in practice.

Among white parents in our sample, there was widespread rejection of the idea that government has a legitimate role to play in desegregating the schools. As table 6–2 shows, over 80 percent of the whites agreed with the statement, "The government has no right to tell you where to send your child to school." Over 60 percent felt that the Supreme Court overstepped its proper boundaries in making decisions about school integration. And while about half of the white respondents agreed that local officials should bow to court decisions, approximately the same percentage felt that their local officials should not do so.

Blacks in our sample tended to have more sanguine views than whites toward the legitimacy of governmental action, although perhaps not to the extent that might have been expected. Table 6–2 shows that black compliers were about evenly divided for and against the proposition that government has a right to tell people where to send their children to school. Roughly two-thirds of the black sample supported the Supreme Court's decision-making function respecting school desegregation; about one-third did not. However, by a landslide of 80 percent, blacks agreed that local officials should do what the courts say about integration. Hence, while many black parents had doubts, most apparently lent specific support to the Supreme Court's role in school desegregation and felt that local officials were bound by court orders to desegregate.

Furthermore, there is clear evidence from both black and white respondents that opinions of "the way desegregation was handled around here" are significantly influenced by general attitudes toward the legitimacy of governmental action. A scale of attitudes toward the right of the government to act in the field was constructed from the three legitimacy items reported in table 6–2. The simple correlation (r) between this scale and opinions of local desegregation was a rather strong .463 for white parents, and a low but still significant .179 for black parents. In general, then, people's diffuse attitudes about the proper scope of governmental activity respecting school desegregation seem to affect their specific support for its implementation locally.

Research by social scientists indicates that the kinds of attitudes we have discussed above are fundamental in the sense that they are usually based on childhood learning in the family and community, tend to change slowly if at all during adult life, and largely determine people's "gut reactions" to specific events and situations. As we have seen, parental views of local desegregation tend to be affected by their basic attitudes toward school desegregation in principle and toward the legitimacy of governmental action in the field. There is little realistic hope that school policymakers can bring about extensive changes in such attitudes, at least in the short run. Yet the problems of policymakers are immediate; and it is hardly helpful to tell officials that they must await long-run improvements in people's basic predispositions before achieving a greater degree of support for local desegregation programs. We turn, then, to analyses of other kinds of factors that may also influence parental support for local desegregation, and over which policymakers have some measure of direct, short-run control.

The Impacts of Desegregation Plan Features

As children experience increasing objective demands from local desegregation plans, subjective support for local implementation programs among their parents might decrease. To investigate this assumption, we will examine the influence of three major plan variables: (1) the percent black enrollment in the child's public school; (2) whether or not the child was bused to school; and (3) the distance in miles between the child's home and school.

Percent Black Enrollment in the Child's School

The relationship between parental approval of local desegregation and the percent black enrollment in the schools is presented in table 6–3. We had expected that for whites, approval of desegregation would decrease with higher black enrollments. This is not the case. With one exception, approval of desegregation among the white sample appears fairly constant across the range of black enrollment. The exception to this pattern occurs among respondents with children in schools between 40 and 50 percent

Table 6–3
Percent Black Enrollment and Percent Approving of Local Desegregation

% Black	*White Complier % Approving*	*Black Complier % Approving*
0–9	27.4	68.2
10–19	26.2	71.2
20–29	33.4	71.8
30–39	25.6	72.0
40–49	12.9	57.2
50+	25.8	72.0

Table 6–4
Change in Percent Black Enrollment (1971–72 to 1972–73) and Percent Approving of Local Desegregation

	Change in Percent Black Enrollment			
	Less than 30% to Less than 30%	*30% or more to Less than 30%*	*Less than 30% to 30% or more*	*30% or more to 30% or more*
White Compliers				
% Approve	29.2	31.0	14.6	25.7
Black Compliers				
% Approve	69.8	72.7	76.2	65.0

black. Approval appears clearly lower within this group, perhaps reflecting the uncertainty and tension associated with the near majority black enrollment of the schools.

The impact of a given level of black concentration on parental attitudes also may be conditioned by previously experienced black concentrations. Parents of a child who was transferred from a school 10 percent black to a school 40 percent black may react more negatively than parents of a child attending a school 40 percent black for the second consecutive year. The effect of change in percent black enrollment on white approval is shown in table 6–4. Quite clearly, reassignment of a child from a school with less than 30 percent black to one with a higher black enrollment depresses approval of local policy. Note further that a movement of the white child in the reverse direction—to a school with proportionally fewer blacks—raises white approval to about the same level as when children remained in heavily white schools over both years. Hence, increased exposure to black children from one year to the next appears to decrease white parental subjective approval of local desegregation, and decreased exposure to blacks over time seems to raise parental support.

The expectation for black respondents is for a curvilinear relationship. Since blacks prefer integrated settings, we would expect approval to be lowest among black parents whose children remain in virtually all black schools despite desegregation in the district. Evidence also suggests, however, that blacks have little desire to be pioneers in all-white settings.[5] We would expect, therefore, lower approval among black parents whose children were assigned to virtually all-white or all-black schools.

The data for black compliers in table 6–4 provide no support for this expectation. As is the case for whites, approval of desegregation in practice is relatively constant at all levels of black enrollment. Also consistent with the findings for whites, there is some decrease in approval among the black respondents whose children are in schools 40 to 50 percent black. Furthermore, the data on change in percent black enrollment in table 6–4 indicate that the attitudes of black compliers are insensitive to temporal shifts in the black enrollment. In sum, none of our analyses supports the argument of segregationists that blacks are more content when their children attend "their own" schools.

Busing

Among whites, busing appears to be positively, albeit weakly, linked to disapproval of the implementation of desegregation. While about 29 percent of the parents of nonbused children approved of the local handling of desegregation, only about 22 percent of the parents of bused children approved. However, this simple relationship requires further analysis. Is the application of busing *per se* a source of disapproval among whites regardless of the racial composition of the assigned public schools, or does it generate disapproval primarily because it exposes the white child to contacts with larger proportions of black schoolmates than occurs in the absence of busing? The latter appears to be the more accurate answer. When the assigned school was less than 30 percent black, the presence or absence of busing did not influence white opinions. However, when the assigned school was more than 30 percent black, whites whose children were bused were more likely to disapprove (84 percent) of the handling of desegregation than those not bused (73 percent). Apparently, then, busing is a source of white parental disapproval not so much for its own sake but because it tends to place the white child in a more heavily black school.

Busing does not appear to affect opinions of local desegregation among black respondents. Blacks approved of the handling of desegregation overwhelmingly whether or not their children were bused and, if bused, whether or not they were transported to schools with higher or lower proportions of black students.

As was the case for the percent black enrollment, the effect of busing may be contingent upon the previous busing experience of the child. This appears to be so particularly among whites. Those whose children were bused for the first time in the year of our interviews had a lower rate of approval (18 percent) than those whose children were bused in both the past and the present year (25 percent). Further, whites whose children had not been bused in either year had a higher rate of approval (29 percent) than either of the latter two groups. Nevertheless, temporal analysis again suggests that white parents object not so much to busing as to the increase in the child's exposure to black children that normally accompanies busing. White compliers with children newly scheduled for busing, but who were assigned to predominantly white schools, approved of local desegregation by approximately 26 percent—near the level for the nonbused group. However, when the new experience of a bus ride was accompanied by an assignment to a school with more than a 30 percent black enrollment (as was more frequently the case), white approval declined to about 13 percent. Thus, all of our analyses indicate that busing *per se* has little direct impact on subjective support, but the onset of busing plus an assignment to a higher percent black school affects support substantially and negatively.

Support for the handling of desegregation was also slightly lower among black compliers whose children experienced the onset of busing (62 percent) than among those whose children were not being bused (68 percent). We assumed that the onset of busing for black children would be associated with an assignment to a predominantly white school, but the data reveal that this assumption was incorrect. Over two-thirds of the black children being bused for the first time were transferred to schools with more than 30 percent black enrollments. Among the latter, parental approval of desegregation was markedly low (57 percent); however, when the onset of busing was accompanied by the placement of the black child in a school less than 30 percent black, support was at a high level (72 percent). Here we must caution the reader not to conclude that black parents would prefer to have their children go to schools with many whites rather than with many blacks. As our analysis unfolds, it will become evident that other variables are involved in the dissatisfaction among blacks with children newly bused to schools with high black enrollment.

Distance

Parents of both races may well be apprehensive when their children are removed from a familiar neighborhood environment and sent to little-known schools in distant parts of town. Furthermore, a long bus ride may require early-morning departures and disturbances of family schedules. Yet school officials may have no alternative but to impose long bus rides on many children to overcome residential segregation. How, then, does the distance from home to school affect subjective support for desegregation in practice?

The relationship between distance and approval of desegregation for both blacks and whites is shown in table 6–5. For whites, approval appears to decline with distance. However, the major difference appears between those white parents with children traveling less than two miles

Table 6–5
Distance and Percent Approving of the Handling of Desegregation

Opinion of Local Desegregation	Distance to Assigned School		
	0–2 miles	*3–10 miles*	*11+ miles*
White Compliers			
% Approve	29.1	23.0	18.9
Black Compliers			
% Approve	69.9	71.5	40.8

and the remainder of the sample. Florida law provides for bus transportation only for students living farther than two miles from school. Thus, much of the apparent impact of distance on white parents' attitudes appears attributable simply to busing as such. Furthermore, as our previous discussion of busing would lead us to expect, the black enrollment in the school is of paramount importance. Approximately, 28 percent of the white compliers with children traveling more than ten miles to school with less than 30 percent black approved of desegregation locally, compared to only 15 percent of those traveling more than ten miles to schools 30 percent or more black.

The influence of distance on black attitudes seems to be exerted only under the extreme condition of busing beyond ten miles. Below this distance, support for school desegregation is relatively constant. Of the black children traveling over ten miles, more than 70 percent attended a school more than 30 percent black. This information provides the clue to understanding our previous finding that black parents with children newly bused to schools with high black enrollments had an unusually high level of dissatisfaction with local desegregation policy. Black dissatisfaction under these conditions is easily interpretable from an individual cost-benefit standpoint. For many of the black children in question were asked to assume the burden of a long-distance bus ride, only to disembark at schools that were very similar in racial composition to those in the neighborhoods where they boarded the bus. Such an arrangement may seem a rational strategy to policymakers concerned with establishing system-wide racial balance, but pointless or even discriminating from the perspective of the individual black parent.

Plan Feature Combinations

So far, we have analyzed the three major plan features one by one in an attempt to discover which of them was the most salient source of parental approval or disapproval of the local handling of desegregation. But we may approach the question of plan feature impacts on parental support from another perspective. Parents may not react so much against a specific plan impact as against the combined application of plan features to their children. For example, it is one thing for a white child to walk a few blocks to a school having a handful of blacks bused to it from other neighborhoods. It may be quite another thing for a white child to be bused for a long distance to a predominantly black school. In the former case, the child is subject to only one plan element (the percent black in the school) and minimally so. In the latter, the child experiences all three to the maximum. We may presume, then, that as plan applications increase in number and severity, parental support undergoes a progressive decline.

Therefore, we analyzed black and white parental support according to all possible second- and third-order combinations of plan effects (or in statistical terms, all interaction effects of plan features). For white parents, increasing the number and severity of plan impacts did not affect support. Rather surprisingly, over and above busing *per se,* a longer bus ride or an assignment to a heavily black school, *or both,* had no additional depressing effects on white support. In other words, any application of busing to white children depressed parental approval of local desegregation; beyond this, however, support was not decreased further by additional plan applications, however stringent. These findings underscore the great symbolic importance that white parents apparently attach to busing *per se,* quite apart from the increased exposure to black children that normally accompanies a bus ride.

The findings for black parents are different. Only the most extreme combination of all three desegregation plan impacts served to depress black approval of the handling of desegregation in the districts. Among those whose children were bused, and who traveled ten miles or more to school, increases in the percent black enrollment were associated with a significantly lower degree of support. However, increases in the percent black enrollment did not generate lower support among blacks whose children were bused a shorter distance.

Why does black support for local desegregation decline precipitously when their children are bused a long way to heavily black schools but not to predominantly white schools? Why is black support unaffected by a shorter bus ride to a school with many black children in attendance? The answer seems clear. The black children in question are not only bused, but also travel far, only to disembark at schools very similar in racial composition to those in the neighborhood where they boarded the bus. To the parents of these children, the costs of the local desegregation plan may far outweigh its benefits. From the standpoint of school decision-makers, such a combination of plan applications may seem reasonable as part of a district-wide approach to achieving a federally acceptable distribution of black and white children in the schools. From the viewpoint of black parents, however, it may well appear not only burdensome but pointless.

Plan Impacts, Attitudes, and Support

As we have seen, increased applications of desegregation plan features are associated with decreased support for the local handling of desegregation. Why is this so? Is it that as plan impacts increase, latent prejudices among whites toward blacks come to the surface and depress their support? Or is it because, aside from basic feelings about integration, increasing plan impacts are seen as an inconvenience of imposition?

Our analyses suggest an element of truth in both interpretations. White compliers were classified into three groups according to their summed scores on the school integration scale—integrationists, ambivalents, and segregationists. We then examined the mean support for local desegregation among these three groups at increasing levels of plan impacts on their children. The results are reported in table 6–6. Reading

Table 6–6
Mean Support for Local Handling of Desegregation among White Integrationists and Segregationists, According to Plan Feature Impacts

	Attitudes toward School Integration in Principle		
Plan Feature Impacts	*Integrationists*	*Ambivalents*	*Segregationists*
Percent black enrollment			
0 to 10	3.02	3.65	4.30
11 to 30	2.91	3.60	4.30
31 and over	3.18	3.78	4.57
	(P is n.s.)	(P<.05)	(P<.01)
Busing			
Not bused	2.87	3.59	4.27
Bused	3.13	3.76	4.55
	(P<.01)	(P<.01)	(P<.01)
Distance, home to school			
0 to 2 miles	2.87	3.57	4.34
3 to 10 miles	3.09	3.76	4.44
11 or more miles	3.36	3.88	4.61
	(P<.05)	(P<.001)	(P is n.s.)

Note: Table entries are mean scores on five-point scale; lower values indicate approval and higher values indicate disapproval of local handling of desegregation.

Note: Figures in parentheses indicate probabilities that means are significantly different from each other (F-test).

across the table, it is clear that whites with integrationist attitudes support district policies more often than the ambivalents, whatever the level of plan impacts. Hence, basic attitudes toward school integration do affect the willingness of parents to endorse local policy. However, reading down the table, it is also clear that increasing desegregation plan impacts tend to reduce the support of parents whether they are integrationists, ambivalents, or segregationists. The attitudinal factor seems the stronger influence on parental approval of the local handling of desegregation, but increasing plan impacts also seem to have a minor, independent influence on the views of parents.

The Influence of Perceived Educational Quality and Discipline

The effects of school desegregation upon the quality of public education and discipline in the schools has been widely and hotly debated by scholars.[6] Whatever the case may be in reality, subjective beliefs about such matters may be a determinant of approval of desegregation in practice. We saw earlier that avoiders were more often dissatisfied with the quality of instruction provided in the public schools than were compliers. Even so, large numbers of compliers as well as avoiders felt that desegregation negatively affected educational programs in the public schools. It may be, then, that subjective support for local desegregation depends upon confidence in the ability of desegregated public schools to carry out their traditional educational functions.

Parental perceptions of the educational performance of desegregated schools were ascertained by asking, "In general, how satisfied are you with the quality of courses and instruction that [child's name] is getting in his/her school?" Responses to this item by race are presented in table 6–7. A majority of both races appear satisfied with the quality of education provided in their children's schools. The black sample, however, was even more satisfied than the white. Over 90 percent of the blacks indicated that they were satisfied, compared to approximately 75 percent of the whites.

The issue of educational quality often seems related in popular discussions to the issue of school discipline and order. Accordingly, we also asked our respondents, "Is discipline a problem in [child's name] school this year?" Again, a majority of both racial samples indicated that discipline had not been a problem (table 6–7). As with quality, blacks were significantly more positive about discipline than were whites. Almost 85 percent of the blacks did not perceive discipline to be a problem, compared to about 60 percent of the whites.

Table 6–7
Perceptions of School Quality and Discipline by Race

	% White Compliers	*% Black Compliers*
School quality?		
Satisfactory	76.6	91.7
Unsatisfactory	23.4	8.3
Is discipline a problem?		
Yes	40.4	15.6
No	59.6	84.4

As we might expect, perceptions of quality and discipline among white compliers are influenced by the percent black enrollment in their children's schools. Among white compliers, perceptions of quality and discipline decreased with increases up to 50 percent black; curiously, however, their perceptions of both conditions become more benign when half or more of the student body was black. This may reflect the operation of cognitive dissonance. The latter term is used by psychologists to refer to the tendency of persons doing things they don't like to alter their opinions to conform to their behavior. For our respondents the pattern might resemble this reasoning: (1) I don't like sending my child to a predominantly black school; (2) I am sending my child to a predominantly black school; (3) I must be satisfied with the quality and discipline in the school.

For black compliers, perceptions of the schools their children attended were unaffected by the percent black enrollment. Black compliers had overwhelmingly complimentary views of their children's schools whatever the ratio of blacks to whites in attendance.

Given the relationship for whites, between percent black enrollment and perceptions of the schools, the black/white ratio may be the original "cause" of parental support for desegregation policy and the relationship between perceptions of school conditions and opinions could be spurious. We may state the causal problem in a policy context. Could improvements in parents' perceptions of school environment, and thereby their support for local implementation, be purchased only at the cost of reducing black enrollments to perhaps unacceptable levels? Or could parental support for desegregation be increased directly by raising the level of public confidence in the qualitative standards in the schools, without major redistributions in the percentages of black children attending them?

To answer these questions the effects of perceptions of quality and discipline on approval of desegregation were examined separately for white compliers with children attending schools of less than, and more than, 30 percent black. The effect of parental perceptions on subjective approval was the same in both groups. The relationship between perceptions of quality and discipline and approval of desegregation, therefore, does not appear to be simply a product of the relationship between percent black enrollment and approval. Or, in policy terms, even if revisions in the black/white ratio among the schools in a district were impossible, approval by white parents of local desegregation policy could be enhanced by measures to raise their confidence in the educational and regulatory standards within the public schools.

The apparent link between perceptions of school quality, discipline, and approval of desegregation among white compliers may also simply reflect their racial prejudice or lack of support for school desegregation in principle. The more prejudiced the parent or the more opposed to the basic idea of school desegregation, the less likely he or she may be to perceive school quality and discipline optimistically. In short, the root problem may lie not so much in parental lack of confidence in the schools as in more deep-seated attitudes.

For whites, it is no surprise to find that long-run attitudes are positively related to views of conditions within the schools. Our measures of racial prejudice, attitudes toward school integration in principle, and the legitimacy of governmental action are all reasonably good predictors of perceptions of the quality of education and discipline in the schools. And, as we have already seen, these attitudes also help to shape white support for desegregation. Nevertheless, it is not true that white beliefs about educational and disciplinary conditions in the schools are mere surface reflections of their deeper attitudes. For, with the impacts of the latter taken into account statistically, white views of the quality of education and discipline in the schools still affect their approval of the handling of desegregation in their districts. Quite simply, whether prejudiced or not, and whether favorable or not toward school desegregation in principle or the legitimacy of governmental action, white beliefs about the caliber of instruction and order in their children's public schools directly and significantly affect their support for desegregation in their communities.

The Process of Desegregation Policymaking and Parental Support

So far, we have portrayed parents somewhat like "consumers" of the desegregation policies presented to them by school officials, as willing or unwilling to "buy" local desegregation—that is, to support it or not—according to their diffuse attitudes toward it and the personal costs and benefits which this "product" of government imposes on them and their children. The consumer analogy has proved helpful in our analyses up to this point, yet it may be an incomplete model of the sources of parental support. For desegregation policies are the outputs of a *political* process of decision-making, and to underscore this point is to cast a different light on the ways that parents may evaluate the handling of desegregation in their districts. That is, parents may approve or disapprove of local policy according to their expectations of how public policies ought to be formulated and their perceptions of whether or not local desegregation policies conformed to those expectations. In short, parents may judge a public policy not only in view of "what it is" but also according to "how it was made."

Most Americans are taught at an early age that they should be informed and active participants in governmental affairs and that public policies should reflect "the will of the people." Of course, this view of the democratic policy process is highly simplistic and ignores a number of countercurrents in American political ideas, such as the protection of minority rights against majority will. It is also true that the seven school districts in our study had no real choice but to follow federal mandates to desegregate. Nevertheless, the populistic notion of policymaking as a simple process of mass inputs and governmental responses seems widespread and durable. Hence, a critical source of parents' support or nonsupport for the local handling of desegregation may lie in their beliefs as to whether or not the decision-making process conformed to the populistic image.

In a number of fields of public policy, increasing calls have been heard for the decentralization of decision-making and for participation in the policymaking process by people who are directly affected.[7] In these fields, the "target groups" of policies are seen as active citizens having a legitimate voice in the decision-making process. Respecting desegregation, however, parents are generally cast in the role of subjects of policies formulated by governmental officials largely insulated from mass pressures. It is beyond the scope of our study to discuss the philosophical merits of the citizen versus subject role respecting desegregation decision-making. Suffice it to note that, as an empirical matter, many parents in our sample seemed to see themselves in a subject role and to resent it. In responding to an open-ended question about why they approved or disapproved of the handling of desegregation in their districts, parents repeatedly echoed the subject theme:

Respondent #0776:
It's out of the people's hands. The government is supposed to be operated for the benefit of the people but it doesn't listen to us. This country is a republic, not a democracy.

Respondent #1049:
There's not much the average citizen can do. The government is going to do what they want no matter what the individual thinks. But I think the local officials did the best they could under the circumstances.

Respondent #1098:
We attended meetings and voiced our opinions but it did no good. We were just wasting our time.

Even among whites who felt that their local officials had no choice and did the best they could, the tone of resentment against a passive subject role was volunteered repeatedly. Occasionally, black parents also perceived themselves in the same vein:

Respondent #0859:
Anything that is pushed just isn't going to work. It was a must and I didn't decide it or anything. Desegregation was forced on us and we had no choice.

Only extremely rarely did any parent, of either race, voice anything resembling an active participant role in desegregation planning. Insofar as our respondents articulated any sense of their place in the political process of desegregation policymaking, it was overwhelmingly in the passive subject role.

The Sense of Political Efficacy

It is difficult to deal confidently with these volunteered responses in systematic analysis. However, one of our closed-ended questions, answered by virtually all respondents, seems conceptually very close to tapping the subject-citizen role differentiation. We asked, "How much influence do you feel people like you have had over school integration in this county?"

The widespread lack of a sense of political efficacy in district desegregation policymaking among white parents is striking. Fully 60 percent of the whites felt that they had no voice at all in the decision process; only about 15 percent believed that they had, at the least, "some" influence. Blacks, however, tended to feel more efficacious. Nearly 60 percent responded that people like themselves had either "some" or "a great deal" of influence, but the remaining 40 percent of the black parents reflect little or no sense of influence over local policymaking. Therefore, whites perceive themselves to play the subject role much more often than blacks, yet a substantial percentage of blacks also feel excluded from the process of desegregation policymaking.

Does the sense of political efficacy affect parental support? The answer is quite clearly in the affirmative. Whether white or black, parents who believed themselves to have an effective voice in the desegregation policy process were more likely to approve the local handling of desegregation than those who thought that they were powerless. The simple correlation (r) between these two variables for white parents was .308 and, for blacks, .250. Nor does this relationship disappear when we take into account parents' basic attitudes toward school integration. Although the statistical associations are reduced in magnitude when controlled for these attitudes, they remain significant.[8] In other words, whether parents are for or against school desegregation in principle, their support rises as they increasingly feel that they play the role of citizens having an effective voice in district policymaking concerning desegregation.

The importance of involving community groups in desegregation planning has been urged in government publications issued as manuals for desegregating school districts: "When the community is involved and understands the plans or has participated in drawing them up, it is more likely to support desegregation of the public schools."[9] Our analysis bears out this assumption. A great many parents of both races felt powerless in the process of district decision-making, but an increasing sense of political efficacy in this process was apparently an important foundation of support for the local handling of desegregation.

School Officials as Influences on Parents' Support

Government manuals for districts undergoing desegregation have stressed not only the need for community involvement but also the potential capacity of local school officials to influence community views toward desegregation. Support may be increased, it is said, through a united front in favor of school integration on the part of district officials: "Thus clear and forthright positions supporting desegregation, both by the superintendent and the board, are important bases for school change."[10] The assumption of "elite influence" on mass opinions also has appeared in scholarly studies of school desegregation. Crain, for example, agrees that community opinions of school integration are shaped by a number of factors but that once local elites formulate a policy,

> . . . public opinion is then more a reaction to the decisions of elites than an independent force. Although the elite anticipation of that reaction may have played an earlier role in the decision, public opinion is heavily influenced by its leadership.[11]

Nevertheless, it should be pointed out that very little careful research has appeared on the degree to which school officials may actually affect community views of desegregation. Hence, the leadership capacity of those who occupy official positions seems more of an assumption than a verified conclusion. Moreover, studies in other policy fields have indicated that the public is generally unaffected by officials' stands on sensitive issues, and it is not clear why the case should be different respecting school desegregation.[12] In any case, the evidence gathered in our seven-county study provides a base for investigating the extent to which officials' positions on school integration were an effective influence on parents' support.

Respondents were asked how the "superintendent of schools" and "most of the school board" in their districts felt about school integration. Responses to these items were precoded "for" and "against" integration, and were summed for each parent. The hypothesis is that as school officials are increasingly seen as favoring school integration, support for the local handling of desegregation will increase.

For whites, the analysis of this relationship does little to bear out the hypothesis; the simple correlation between support for local desegregation and perceptions of elites was very low (.184). For blacks, on the other hand, the correlation was fairly substantial (.398). These simple relationships suggest that parents increasingly tend to support local desegregation as they perceive local officials to favor it. Yet this finding needs further study, for a great deal of research in social science has indicated that people often project their own views on public officials.[13] So, for example, a staunch segregationist parent may take it for granted that officials share his racial views, while a committed integrationist parent may project his predispositions on the same officials. And to the extent that such projection effects occur, school officials do not exercise any genuine causal impact on parental support. Hence, the simple relationship reported above must be retested, taking parents' own attitudes toward school integration into account.

Consider, for example, parents whose responses to the attitudinal items indicated that they were personally opposed to school integration. This group can be further subdivided according to whether they felt that local officials were for, or against, school integration. If the "official influence" assumption is valid, we would predict that parents who perceive local officials as favoring integration would themselves support it—at least more often than parents who perceive officials as against school integration. And the same method of analysis applies to parents who were personally sympathetic to integration: those who see officials as antiintegrationist should have lower support scores than those who feel that officials are prointegrationist. Controlling for respondents own attitudes in this manner, is there any remaining residue of influence on parental support stemming from their perceptions of official positions?

For whites, the application of the control for personal attitudes leaves very little left of the relationship between perceptions of official positions and support for local desegregation. In fact, the correlation nearly approaches zero (.061) after white respondents' personal attitudes are taken into account. In short, white parents' support for local desegregation is almost totally unaffected by their views of official positions on the issue.

At first glance, the capacity for official influence upon black parents appears greater. Applying the control procedures outlined above, the association between perceptions of officials and support for local desegregation among blacks remains rather high (.377). Nevertheless, it is hard to believe that, after generations of discrimination, blacks are willing to accept the leadership of the predominantly white school officialdom. In fact, further data analysis suggests that black perceptions of official positions are affected by the local desegregation plan impacts on their children. That is, blacks whose children bear a heavy burden from the implementation plan seem to infer that officials are opposed to desegregation, while those whose children experience lighter plan impacts tend to see officials as more favorable to desegregation.

Putting It All Together: The Determinants of Parental Support

The long-run success or failure of desegregation as a public policy may depend very largely upon community beliefs and values, and perhaps especially those of parents of children attending desegregated schools. Nonsupport among complying parents may have serious consequences for integrated education—motivational and disciplinary problems among school children, interracial violence, and a weakened financial base. Among most of the whites in our sample, behavioral compliance signified as much an inability to pay private school tuitions as a positive outlook on desegregated schooling. Hence, local school policymakers have the dual problem of maintaining an acceptable quantitative balance of black and white children in the schools while, at the same time, building community attitudinal support for district desegregation. Lacking the latter, the achievement of the former may be a hollow victory. What, then, might local district officials do to minimize community opposition to school desegregation?

Our analyses in this chapter have suggested the strong causal impact on parents' support of their fundamental attitudes toward school integration and the legitimacy of governmental action to desegregate the schools. As these attitudes become more favorable, support for local desegregation increases. Yet our data also suggest a strong wave of attitudinal opposition among white parents both to school integration in principle and government's right to implement it. Moreover, there is probably little that school policymakers alone can do to alter such community attitudes, at least in the short run. True, there may be reason to believe that, in time, desegregated school systems may become accepted as routine practice. Yet such optimistic portents for the future are cold comfort for policymakers facing lack of public support for school desegregation here and now. Given the fact that so many whites are attitudinally hostile to desegregation, are there any more immediate steps policymakers might take to increase parental support for the handling of desegregation in their school districts?

We have dealt with several possible determinants of parental support over which school policymakers may have some measure of direct control or influence—objective plan applications to children, impressions of school quality and discipline, community involvement in desegregation decision-making, and official leadership. However, these factors have been considered in a "one by one" manner, without putting them all together in a simultaneous analysis. We may utilize a multivariate statistical technique (multiple regression) which, in effect, forces each of these factors to compete against all the rest as predictors of variations in parental support. By using this technique, we may isolate the most salient of all the hypothesized sources and discover which (if any) fall by the wayside as significant determinants of support.

Let us first consider the results of the multi-variate procedure for white compliers (see table 6–8). It reveals that basic attitudes toward school integration were, by far, the most powerful predictors of support for this group of parents. The combined force of all the rest of the variables together did not diminish the predictive strength of the attitudinal factor.

The desegregation plan features did not emerge from the multi-variate analysis as important determinants of white support. Only one of the three plan elements—busing—produced a statistically significant effect on support; the causal influence of the percent black enrollment and of the distance from home to school diminished to virtually zero. Furthermore, the joint application of all three plan elements had surprisingly little impact on white approval of local desegregation.[14] That is, over and above busing *per se,* a longer bus ride or an assignment to a heavily black school, *or both,* had no additional depressing effects on white support. Even this heaviest possible burden from the desegregation plan had no discernible impact on parental support. The sources of the latter clearly lie elsewhere.

Next to the attitudinal factor, the most important determinant of white parents' support was their sense of political efficacy with regard to local desegregation policymaking. Taking into account all of the other

Table 6–8
Support for the Handling of Desegregation: Multiple Correlation and Regression Analysis

	White Compliers				Black Compliers			
Independent Variables	*(b)*	*(beta)*	*(s)*	*(F)*	*(b)*	*(beta)*	*(s)*	*(F)*
Attitude toward school integration	.568	.312	.039	209.80[a]	.089	.035	.076	1.37
Percent black enrollment	−.052	−.031	.036	2.06	.065	.031	.063	1.06
Busing	−.162	−.069	.049	10.92[a]	−.010	−.005	.068	.02
Distance bused	−.009	−.038	.004	3.32	−.002	−.015	.003	.26
Perceived quality of education	.125	.098	.028	19.20[a]	.166	.114	.045	13.66[a]
Perceived discipline in school	.225	.093	.054	17.34[a]	.187	.063	.091	4.18[c]
Political efficacy	.187	.162	.035	28.71[a]	.228	.161	.030	56.04[a]
Perceptions of officials' positions	.052	.060	.018	8.14[b]	.209	.274	.023	81.83[a]

Dependent Variables	White Compliers	Black Compliers
Mean (5-point scale)	2.290	3.315
Standard deviation	1.218	1.172
F-ratio	66.042	21.067
Standard error of estimate	1.034	1.041
Number of respondents	1184	581
R^2	.224	.149

F-test:

[a]$P < .001$.

[b]$P < .01$.

[c]$P < .05$.

predictor variables, efficacy remained a major source of parental support. However, the other "political process" variable—perceptions of official commitment to desegregation—was at best a marginally significant contributor to white support. Hence, the analysis of these two "political process" variables portrays a white public who overwhelmingly feel powerless to influence desegregation and who, for this reason, disapprove of its handling. It is also a public whose degree of support for local policy is very largely impervious to the influence of local school officials.

Finally, white perceptions of the educational quality and the discipline in their children's schools continue to exert a robust influence on support, even after all the other variables are taken into account in the multi-variate analysis. Regardless of the basic attitudes of whites, their views of the decision-making process or of the impact of plan features, parental support for local desegregation increases as the schools are increasingly believed to carry out their traditional functions.

For black parents, the variable which emerges as most salient in predicting support is the perception of the stand of local officials on the school integration issue. Yet, for reasons indicated previously, it is hard to believe that the predominantly white school officialdom in the study districts were opinion leaders in the black community. In fact, another look at the data suggests that black perceptions of official feelings about integration stems from desegregation plan impacts. That is, blacks whose children bear a heavy burden from the plan tend to believe that local officials are hostile to school integration. And, as noted previously, heavy desegregation plan impacts undermine black support for the handling of desegregation in their districts. Hence, it remains very doubtful that school officials can effectively act as leaders of community opinion regarding desegregation policy.

Setting aside the "official influence" hypothesis, the sense of political efficacy becomes the most powerful predictor of black support for the handling of desegregation. As with whites, positive views of the local handling of desegregation among blacks tend to be rooted in the belief that one plays the citizen rather than the subject role in desegregation policymaking. Finally, the multi-variate analyses indicate another similarity between the bases of support among blacks and whites; in both groups, policy approval increases as there is a growing confidence in the educational quality and discipline within the public schools.

Unlike the case for whites, attitudes toward school integration are not a significant contributor to black support. However, this finding is almost surely a statistical artifact lacking any real substantive meaning, for reasons we have outlined previously. Since black attitudes toward integration in principle vary so little, there is no way to relate differences in this factor to differences in support. Assuming a sample of black respondents having a greater variation in basic attitudes, it seems very likely that the latter would emerge as a strong underpinning for policy support.

Finally, neither busing, the distance bused, nor the percent black enrollment were significant predictors of black support for local desegregation. But we find clear and strong evidence that the most extreme combination of the three plan impacts seriously depressed black opinions of the handling of desegregation. While the three plan features taken one by one have no bearing on support, the combination of a long bus ride and an assignment to a heavily black school is a strong negative influence on black support.

On the whole, then, the sources of support and nonsupport for local desegregation policy are not very different for black and white parents, except in the case of desegregation plan applications. White parents' support is undermined when their children are subjected to busing, but additionally heavy plan impacts do not further depress white support appreciably. In contrast, blacks seem not to object to any but the most burdensome combination of objective policy impacts. But again, aside from this difference between blacks and whites, desegregation policymakers face much the same kinds of problems in attempting to build support in both groups of parents.

What, then, might policymakers do to raise the level of community support for desegregation policies? Our analyses indicate that marginal increases in white support could be realized by reducing the busing of white children to the minimum consistent with the implementation of biracial schooling. On the other hand, officials might impose desegregation plan elements upon black children without fearing a loss of black parental support—except that the most extreme combination of plan elements should be avoided. Nevertheless, compared with other determinants of support, the plan feature applications are not a very important determinant of how parents feel about the handling of desegregation in their districts. For this reason, the reduction of plan applications to children cannot be expected to produce major gains in community support.

Also, there is no convincing evidence that local school officials could increase support for school desegregation by taking public stands in favor of it. Parents are very likely to project their own viewpoints upon school officials, and, as we saw, even with such projection effects removed, perceptions of official views had, at best, only trace effects on parental support for local desegregation.

The only leadership strategy that holds much promise of increasing community support is one that actively engages parents in the process of desegregation policymaking. Such an "interactive" leadership strategy would facilitate and even encourage parental inputs into local decision-making, accommodate parental inputs to federally permissible alternatives, and, in general, reduce the distance between the parent and the decision-making process. This strategy, in short, emphasizes the citizen role of parents over the subject role often assigned them in the past.

Finally, it is clear from our data that many parents of both races are concerned about the quality of education and order in the public schools, and that these concerns are not mere symptoms of racist thinking. Moreover, doubts of parents about the quality and order of their children's schools are a major source of nonsupport for the handling of desegregation. Of course, public concern about "why Johnny can't read" was widespread long before the advent of desegregation, but parental judgments of the latter are not separate and apart from their judgments of the quality of their children's schools. Hence, serious efforts by policymakers to improve the schools' performance of their traditional educational functions should lead to a strengthened community support for desegregation policies.

The implementation of these strategies to improve parental support for desegregation will not be easy or cheap. Nevertheless, they may be well worth their costs when measured against the baneful consequences of continued public nonsupport for district desegregation policies.

Notes

1. Micheal W. Giles, Douglas S. Gatlin, and Everett F. Cataldo, "Parental Support for School Referenda," *Journal of Politics,* 38 (May 1976), 442–51.

2. Nancy H. St. John, *School Desegregation: Outcomes for Children* (New York: John Wiley and Sons, 1975), pp. 64–65, 89–91.

3. *Gallup Opinion Index,* October 1973; Report No. 100, 14.

4. Arthur H. Miller and Jack Citrin, "Political Issues and Trust in Government," *American Political Science Review,* 68 (September 1974), 951–72.

5. Thomas F. Pettigrew, "Attitudes on Race and Housing: A Social-Psychological View," in Amos H. Hawley and Vincent P. Rock, eds., *Segregation in Residential Areas* (Washington: National Academy of Sciences, 1973), pp. 52–53.

6. James S. Coleman and others, *Equality of Racial Opportunity* (Washington: U.S. Government Printing Office, 1967). Also see Thomas F. Pettigrew, *Racially Separate or Together?* (New York: McGraw-Hill Publishing Co., 1971). A helpful summary and critique of much of this research is found in St. John, *School Desegregation . . . ,* especially Chapter 6.

7. A useful overview of decentralization and participation in policymaking is contained in *Public Administration Review,* XXXII (October 1972), Special Issue: "Curriculum Essays on Citizens, Politics, and Administration in Urban Neighborhoods."

8. The second-order partial correlation between efficacy and support, controlling for attitudes toward legitimacy and school integration, is .133, which is significant at .001.

9. Mark A. Chesler, Judith Guskin, and Phyllis Erenberg, *Planning Educational Change: Vol. II, Human Resources in School Desegregation* (Washington: U.S. Department of Health, Education, and Welfare, Office of Education, 1969), p. 19.

10. Ibid.

11. Robert L. Crain and others, *Design for a National Longitudinal Study of School Desegregation: Vol. 1, Issues in Theory and Method* (Santa Monica, California: Rand Corp., September, 1974), p. vi.

12. David O. Sears and Richard E. Whitney, *Political Persuasion* (Morristown, N.J.: General Learning Press, 1973). Also see Howard D. Hamilton, "Direct Legislation: Some Implications of Open Housing Referenda," *American Political Science Review,* 64 (March 1970), 124–37.

13. An introduction and summary of cognitive balance theory is presented in David Krech, Richard S. Crutchfield, and Egerton L. Ballachey, *Individual in Society* (New York: McGraw-Hill Book Co., Inc., 1962), pp. 38–46.

14. Interaction terms were obtained by multiplying the appropriate plan variables.

7 Desegregation and Educational Planning

What are the main policy implications to be drawn from the preceding chapters? It seems clear that the effectiveness of desegregation is linked closely to the scope and timing of the remedy, and to the attendant costs of noncompliance by parents with children in school. The practicality or feasibility of metropolitan or area-wide desegregation has been debated widely by jurists, educational planners, and the media since the Richmond and Detroit school desegregation cases. The opinion often expressed is that metropolitan plans might not prove workable even if constitutional grounds were established for including both city and suburban schools in the remedies. Presumably the requirement for suburban children to attend inner-city schools, the need to transport large numbers of students over considerable distances, and the substantial reorganization of the schools themselves would be met by stiff resistance and would prove too difficult to manage.

One of the contributions of this study is that this debate need no longer be carried out entirely in a vacuum. The conditions that have been presumed to mitigate against area-wide desegregation planning were precisely the conditions under which desegregation was implemented with apparent success in our study districts. In each instance, desegregation occurred on a county-wide basis. The number of students transported to school was substantial and considerable distances were involved. One district in particular required students who resided in the suburban area or the urban fringe to spend some years in inner-city schools. To be sure, avoidance of desegregation occurred in these districts; but it was neither stiff nor massive. The vast majority of parents complied with desegregation by keeping their children in public schools.

It might be argued that the seven school districts were able to overcome obstacles to desegregation because they possessed special attributes or certain characteristics not found in school districts elsewhere. The districts had always been county-wide. Many students in those districts may have been accustomed to riding a bus because transportation was employed to maintain segregation. Southern whites may have become resigned to the inevitable after years of struggle to prevent desegregation; and desegregation may have come more easily to southern whites long accustomed to a black population in their presence. The absence of a private school tradition in the South may have limited the availability of the private school alternative in the seven districts.

A reconsideration of information presented earlier in this book does not show that the seven districts were particularly unique in these respects or that the ascribed characteristics paint an accurate picture of the districts. Desegregation resulted in a significant increase in student transportation in the four districts for which we had complete information. In only one of them were the pre-desegregation and post-desegregation busing levels approximately the same. Consequently, many students were experiencing busing for the first time with the advent of school desegregation. The districts were located, of course, in a southern state. However, many of the families living there (40 percent) did not have southern origins, and the rate of compliance among nonsouthern parents did not differ appreciably from that of southern parents. Finally, Florida has a stronger private school tradition than any other southern state except Louisiana. In 1973–74, there were nearly 300 private schools and 627 public schools in the seven districts. On average, then, there was one private school for about every two public schools in each district, providing ample opportunity, it would seem, to select the private school alternative.

It is true that the districts had been county-wide for many years, and it may be quite another matter to implement desegregation successfully when a number of separate, independent school districts have to be consolidated as a condition for area-wide implementation of desegregation. Our data suggest, however, that the metropolitan remedy may be workable even under such a condition. Recall that the most important desegregation plan feature contributing to avoidance among whites was a threshold of 30 percent black in the assigned school. In metropolitan areas black enrollments are typically far higher in central city schools than in suburban schools. Thus a desegregation plan for city schools alone would result in white students attending schools with higher black concentrations than a plan including both city and suburban schools. In most metropolitan areas a city-suburban remedy could reduce racial balances in the schools below the critical 30 percent black threshold. More students might have to be transported but the incidence and distance of busing do not contribute appreciably to avoidance. A metropolitan remedy, therefore, could conceivably produce a lower incidence of avoidance than a city-only remedy.

The factors associated with large scale, area-wide desegregation stir negative sentiments among parents. These negative sentiments have relatively little influence over behavior but apparently undercut attitudinal support for school desegregation. Parents in our seven districts could be classified into three groups. At one end were compliers who did not object to school desegregation or the means necessary to achieve it. Most of them were black. At the other end were avoiders who objected to desegregation by whatever means. Virtually all of them were white. Between those polar opposites were the vast majority of white parents who complied although they complained about busing and had reservations about educational quality in desegregated public schools. They may have been reluctant, but they allowed their children to attend those schools nevertheless. Perhaps it has become necessary to develop policies governing controversial issues in such a fashion as to exact behavioral compliance first and to work out the problem of diffuse support later. While such a procedure runs counter to the popular notion that in a political democracy important policies should rest on a firm foundation of public support, it is also true that restoration of individuals' constitutional rights to equal treatment under the law is not determined by public opinion. The entire history of school desegregation demonstrates that if we were still waiting for mass opinion to swing behind the doctrines enunciated by the U.S. Supreme Court in the *Brown* decisions we might still be waiting for the first school to desegregate. From a public policy standpoint it is doubtless fortunate that most white parents have complied with desegregation even if reluctantly and against their attitudinal preferences. Clearly school desegregation is a policy issue in which mass attitudes have not governed behavior. Perhaps behavioral change will produce attitudinal change so that behavioral compliance with desegregation may eventually be accompanied by attitudinal support for it.

While the findings of this study indicate that such a match between attitudes and behavior has yet to be made, they also suggest some ways by which that objective may be achieved. The most important one would be a reduction of the distance and a change in the relationship between parents and officials in the policy-making process. Lip service is often paid by local officials to the involvement of parents in desegregation planning. Lately some federal district courts have appointed community-based monitoring boards to supervise implementation of desegregation. But most often, parental participation is absent at the formulation stage when the plans are actually being developed. Because school officials very often delay complying with court orders as long as they can, there is little time for a participatory process to occur and parents may not even know what schools their children have been assigned to attend until the school year is about to begin. In one of our districts, parents were uninformed about their children's school assignments practically to the last minute. School officials never communicated directly with parents to inform them of their children's assignments. About one week before the opening of school an official announcement of changes in school attendance boundaries and busing schedules was published in the local newspaper. Parents who saw the paper and had some map reading skills could find out where to send their children to school. Those who did not deluged the school board office with telephone inquiries. Little wonder that parents resented the subject role to which they had been relegated and disapproved of the handling of desegregation locally.

By contrast, an emphasis on the citizen or participant role for parents would produce timely interaction between officials and parents, accommodate parental inputs into the desegregation process, and make desegregation planning a mutually reinforcing partnership between officials and affected parents. Once parents play the role of active participants rather than passive recipients, their objections and resentments may correspondingly decline. To build community support, courts and school officials should provide for parental participation at the formulation stage of desegregation policy rather than at the implementation stage when a good deal of potential support may have been dissipated.

What else may be done at the official level to build community support? We have seen that parents labor under considerable misinformation about the educational effects of desegregation. Many have doubts about the quality of education provided by desegregated schools and believe that the achievement levels of white students are adversely affected despite considerable evidence to the contrary. Such doubts and misinformation must be dispelled and corrected. Participation in desegregation planning should help to build confidence in the schools and provide correct information. Beyond that, desegregation should be viewed essentially as an educational process. A desegregation plan containing only the logistics for achieving racial balances in the schools is incomplete. In the end it is the educational payoff that counts; and all parents need to be reassured that there is, indeed, an educational product within an orderly learning environment at the end of the bus ride. Such reassurances can be provided if school systems make detailed educational objectives and the means to accomplish them an integral part of their desegregation plans. That would involve a careful assessment of the educational needs of students, a plan to develop the capacity of the school system to meet those needs, and the establishment of an evaluation system to determine progress toward educational goals. Such a process is beyond the capacity of upper level school administrators and court officials alone because they have neither the capacity nor, apparently, the credibility to do the job themselves. A coordinated and cooperative effort involving official actors, parents, teachers, and students themselves should be required to insure that the bottom line of desegregation is not simply whether students attend their assigned schools, but whether those schools acceptably perform the functions for which students are attending them. Over the past twenty years desegregation has often been viewed as an onerous burden carried by the majority on behalf of minority students. Desegregation can also provide an opportunity to refresh the mission of the public schools to provide an education of quality for all students. If that is done there is a good chance that the necessary consistency between constitutional imperatives and public preferences can be achieved.

Index

Academic image, of desegregated schools, 4–5, 45–49, 63–67, 68
Accreditation, and school quality, 63
Administrators: effect of extrasystem avoidance on, 5, 48; influence of, on parental support, 89–91; role of, in school integration, 44, 101–102
Alston, Jon P., 38, 57
Ambivalents, reaction of, to desegregation plan impacts, 83–84
Area-wide desegregation, 99. *See also* County school systems
Atlanta's public schools, extrasystem avoidance in, 4
Attendance zones, school: altering of, for desegregation, 18, 19, 54; Florida's requirement of segregated, 15–16; and intrasystem avoidance, 2; research on racial changes in, 6–7. *See also* Neighborhoods; Residential moves
Attitudes: of blacks toward desegregation policies, 71–73; toward busing policies, 42, 71–72, 79–80; toward class prejudice, 39–41; toward desegregation in principle, 73–75; toward legitimacy of desegregation policy, 43–44, 75–77; toward public education, 45–47, 63–67, 84–86; toward racial prejudice, 38–39; toward school integration, 41–43; toward school officials, 44–45, 89–91; toward self efficacy, 44, 88–89, 92–93; similarity of complier and avoider, 48–49; in South toward blacks, 37–38
Avoidance: and attitudes toward public officials, 44–45, 49; and busing policies, 42, 54–56; clarifications of, 9–11; and costs of desegregation, 53–54; educational implications of, 4–5, 45–49; extrasystem, 2, 3, 4–5, 7 (*see also* Private schools); in Florida after desegregation implementation, 24–27; ideas to minimize, 9–11, 68–69; intersystem, 2, 3–4, 7; intrasystem, 1–2, 2–3, 7; and location of school, 60–63; and negative attitude toward desegregation, 41–44; and participation in public education, 45–47; and percent black enrollment, 57–59; potential for, 67–68; and previous status and condition of school, 59–60; and process of resegregation, 2–4; profiles of, 48–49; and racial and class prejudice, 38–41, 50; and regional origin, 37–38; and religious affiliation, 25–26, 37; research on, 5–9; and school quality, 63–67; and social status, 5, 35–37, 48–49. *See also* Compliers
Avoiders: attitudes of, toward busing policies, 42, 54–55; attitudes of, toward legitimacy of desegregation policy, 43–44; attitudes of, toward racial and class prejudice, 38–41, 48; attitudes of, toward school integration, 41–43; black, 72; and location of schools, 60–63; methods of selecting sample groups of, 31–33; nonsouthern migrants as, 38, 48; opinion of school quality, 63–67, 84; participation of, in demonstrations, 50; past commitment of, to public schools, 45–47; and percent black enrollment, 57–59; and perception of desegregation costs, 53–54; potential, 67–68; and previous

status and condition of school, 59–60; procedures for conducting interviews with, 33–34; religious affiliations of, 25–26, 37; response rate of, to interviews, 34; sense of efficacy of, 44; social status of, 35–37, 48; trust of school officials, 44–45; weakening support of, for public schools, 48–49. *See also* Compliers; Parents

Baltimore, Maryland, study of desegregation in, 6, 57
Beshers, James M., 39
Blacks: alternative schools for, 71, 72; class prejudice against, 39, 40; effects of class segregation in education on, 5, 36, 48–49; percent school enrollments of, and avoidance, 57–59; racial prejudice against, 37–38, 38–39, 40. *See also* Compliers; Parents, black
''Black separatism,'' and desegregation policy, 71, 72, 73
Blalock, Hubert, 39
Brown v. *Board of Education,* 1, 15, 16, 18, 101
Busing: as costly obstacle to compliance, 54–56, 92; distance traveled and approval of desegregation policy, 80–81; and exposure to higher percent black in schools, 79–80; parental objections to, 42, 79–80, 81–84; problems with, in county school systems, 20–21; rates for schools in Florida, 23–24; target-area, 18, 20, 21

Catholic parochial schools, growth of, in Florida, 25–27, 37. *See also* Private schools
Central city schools: effects of desegregation on, 3–4, 7; high percent black enrollment in, 100
Characteristics, school. *See* School characteristics
''Christian academies,'' growth of, in Florida, 25–27. *See also* Private schools
Citizen role vs. subject role, of parents in desegregation policies, 86–91, 96
Civil Rights Act of 1964, 1
Class prejudice: and avoidance, 39–41, 48; effect of, on public education, 5, 36, 48–49.
Clotfelter, Charles, 8–9, 36
Clustering technique, of desegregation, 17, 18, 21
Cognitive dissonance, in perceptions of school quality, 85
Coleman, James S., 3, 6, 8, 35
Collins, Leroy, 16
Compliance, parental perceptions of costs of, 53–54. *See also* Avoidance
Compliers: attitudes of, toward busing policies, 42, 54–55, 79–80; attitudes of, toward legitimacy of desegregation policy, 43–44, 75–77; attitudes of, toward racial and class prejudice, 38–41; attitudes of, toward school integration, 41–43, 73–75; commitment of, to public schools, 45–47; determinants for support of, 71–72, 91–96 (*see also* Support, parental); inability of, to afford private school alternative, 67–68; and location of school, 60–63, 80–81; methods of selecting sample groups of, 31–33; nonsouthern migrants as, 38, 48; opinion of school quality, 63–67, 84–86; participation of, in demonstrations, 50; and percent black enrollment, 57–59, 77–79; perception of desegregation costs, 53–54; and previous status and condition of school, 59–60; procedures for conducting inter-

views with, 33–34; reactions of, to desegregation plan impacts, 81–84, 82; religious affiliations of, 37; responses of, to implementation of desegregation, 72–73; response rate of, to interviews, 34; sense of efficacy of, 44, 88–89; social status of, 35–37; trust of school officials, 44–45, 89–91. *See also* Avoiders; Parents; Parents, black; Parents, white

Costs, of school desegregation policies, 9–11, 53–54, 68–69; busing policies, 42, 54–56, 79–80; percent black enrollment, 57–59, 77–79; previous status and condition of school, 59–60; school discipline and safety, 66–67, 84–86; school location, 60–63, 80–81; school quality, 63–66, 84–86

County school systems, 99, 100; difficulties in desegregation of, 20–21; and extrasystem avoidance, 4; Florida's use of, 15; private school alternative in, 24–27; study of desegregation in, 16–20

Crain, Robert L., 35, 89

Dade County, Florida: increase of private school enrollment in, 24–27; racial balances of schools in, 21–23; study of desegregation implementation in, 16–17; use of busing in, 23, 54

Dayton case, 5

Demonstrations, parents participating in, 50

Desegregation policymaking. *See* Policymaking, desegregation

Discipline, school. *See* School discipline

Distance, school. *See* School distance

Downs, Anthony, 44

Duval County, Florida, 53, 62; busing rates for schools in, 23–24; increase of private school enrollment in, 24–27; problems with long distance busing in, 21; racial balances of schools in, 21–23; study of desegregation implementation in, 17–18

Efficacy: and avoidance, 44; and parental support, 88–89, 92–94

Elementary and Secondary Education Act of 1965, 1

"Elite influence," of school officials, 89–91, 101–102

Elite noncompliance, to desegregation in South, 1

Enrollment data: comparison of, to sample groups, 32–33; on desegregated public schools in Florida, 16–20, 21–23; percent black, and avoidance, 57–59; percent black, and parental support, 77–79; on private schools in Florida, 24–27; research on cause of declining white, 6–9. *See also* Percent black enrollment

Escambia County, Florida: busing rates for schools in, 23–24; private school enrollment in, 24–27; racial balance of schools in, 21–23; study of desegregation implementation in, 19

Extrasystem avoidance. *See* Avoidance

Farley, Reynolds, 7–8, 35

Fitzgerald, Michael R., 7–8

Florida: county school systems of, 15; effects of desegregation on public schools in, 20–24; nonsouthern migrants residing in, 38, 48, 100; private school movement in, 24–27; state's mandate for segregated education, 15–16; study of desegregation implementation in,

16–20. *See also specific study districts*
Florida Educational Directory, 24
Foster, Gordon, 24
"Freedom of choice" plan, of desegregation, 4, 16, 18
Fundamentalist churches, growth of private schools affiliated with, 25–26, 37
Funding, school. *See* School funding

Gallup Poll survey data, 38, 54
Governmental action, legitimacy of, parental attitudes toward, 43–44, 75–77, 86–91
Grade-a-year plan, of desegregation, 18
Greeley, Andrew, 38

Income: comparison of avoider and complier, 36; and potential of avoidance, 67–68
Indianapolis case, 5
Integrationists, reaction of, to desegregation plan impacts, 83–84
Intersystem avoidance. *See* Avoidance
Interviews, parental: procedures for conducting, 33–34; sampling procedures for, 31–32; survey instruments for, 33
Intrasystem avoidance. *See* Avoidance

Kelley, Jonathan, 42
Knapp, Melvin J., 38, 57

Lachman, M. Leanne, 44
Lee County, Florida, 53; busing in, 21, 23; increase of private school enrollment in, 24–27; racial balance of schools in, 21–23; study of desegregation implementation in, 19–20
Leon County, Florida: busing rates for schools in, 23–24; increase of private school enrollment in, 24–27; racial balance of schools in, 21–23; study of desegregation implementation in, 19
Location, school. *See* School location

Manatee County, Florida, 53; busing for schools in, 23; increase of private school enrollment in, 24–27; racial balance of schools in, 21–23; study of desegregation implementation in, 20
Metropolitan desegregation, 99, 100. *See also* County school systems
Mississippi, extrasystem avoidance in, 4, 8, 9
Mobile, Alabama, intrasystem avoidance in, 3
Morgan, David R., 7–8

National Analysts, Inc., 33–34
National Opinion Research Center, 38
Neighborhoods: parental preference of schools in, 42, 54–55; percent black in school, and avoidance, 60–63; research on racial change in, 6–7. *See also* Attendance zones; Residential moves
New York Times, survey on private schools, 4

Pairing technique, of desegregation, 17, 19
Palm Beach County, Florida: busing rates for schools in, 23–24; increase of private school enrollment in, 24–27; problems with target-area busing in, 21; racial balance of schools in, 21–23; study of desegregation implementation in, 18
Parents: attitudes of, toward legitimacy of governmental action, 43–44, 75–77; attitudes of, toward school integration, 41–43, 44, 73–75; citizen role vs. subject role of, 86–91, 96; desegregation plan impacts, effect on support of, 81–84; determinants for support of, 91–96, 101–102; feelings toward school officials, 44–45, 89–91; methods of selecting sample groups of, 31–32; objections to school locations, 60–63;

80–81; and overestimation of percent black enrollments, 54, 59; participation of, in demonstrations, 50; participation of, in public education, 45–47; and perception of desegregation costs, 53–54; as potential avoiders, 67–68; procedures for conducting interviews with, 33–34; racial and class prejudice of, 38–41; reactions of, to busing, 42, 54–56, 79–80; reactions of, to process of desegregation policymaking, 86–91; response rate of, to interviews, 34. *See also* Avoiders; Compliers; Support, parental

Parents, black: attitudes of, toward desegregation in principle, 73–75; attitudes of, toward legitimacy of governmental action, 75–77; attitudes of, toward percent black enrollment in schools, 77–79; as avoiders, 72; basic attitudes of, toward desegregation, 72; desegregation plan impacts, effect on support of, 81–84, 92; determinants for support of, 91–96; reactions of, to busing policies; 79–80; reactions of, to process of desegregation policymaking, 86–88; responses of, to implementation of local desegregation, 72–73; responses of, to school distances, 80–81; responses of, to school quality and discipline, 84–86; school officials' influence on support of, 89–91; sense of political efficacy of, 88–89, 92–93. *See also* Blacks; Compliers

Parents, white: attitudes of, toward desegregation in principle, 73–75; attitudes of, toward legitimacy of governmental action, 75–77; attitudes of, toward percent black enrollment in schools, 77–79; desegregation plan impacts, effect on support of, 81–84, 92; determinants for support of, 91–96; reactions of, to busing policies, 79–80; reactions of, to process of desegregation policymaking, 86–88; responses of, to implementation of local desegregation, 72–73; responses of, to school distances, 80–81; responses of, to school quality and discipline, 84–86; school officials' influence on support of, 89–91, 94; sense of political efficacy of, 88–89; 92–93. *See also* Avoiders; Compliers

Percent black enrollment: avoiders' and compliers' response to, 57–59, 100; black and white parents' response to, 77–79; and perception of quality of school instruction, 85–86. *See also* Enrollment data; Racial balances

Pettigrew, Thomas F., 35

Policymaking: academic research for, 5–9; determinants for parental support of, 91–96; effects of process of, on parental support, 86–88; ideas for effective, 9–11, 68–69; parental questioning of legitimacy of, 43–44, 75–77; parents' sense of political efficacy in, 88–89; primary goal of, 1; school officials' influence on parental support of, 89–91

Private schools: affiliations of, with fundamentalist churches, 37; black attendance of, 72; Catholic parochial schools, 25–26; "Christian academies," 25–26; and decline in value of public education, 5, 45–47, 48, 63–67; as extrasystem avoidance, 2, 4; growth of, in desegregated Florida, 24–27; quality of, 63–64; and social status, 5, 35–37, 67–68; in South, 4, 8, 99. *See also* Avoidance

Public education: commitment of parents to, 45–47; effect of avoidance on quality of, 4–5, 45–49; parental opinion on quality of, 63–67, 84–86, 96. *See also* Avoidance; Private schools
Public officials: influences of, on parental support, 89–91, 94; parental trust of, 44–45; role of, in desegregation implementation, 101

Quality, school. *See* School quality

Racial balances: effect of, on amount of avoidance, 57–59; in Florida's county school systems, 21–23; research on changes in, during school desegregation, 5–9. *See also* Enrollment data; Percent black enrollment
Racial prejudice: of avoiders and compliers, 38–39, 40, 48; and perception of effectiveness of desegregation plan, 59, 73, 83–84, 86, 92; regional differences in, 37–38
Religious affiliations, of avoiders and compliers, 25–26, 37
Resegregation, and avoidance, 2–4
Residential moves: research on cause and effect of, 6–7; and resegregation, 2, 3, 4, 5; and social status, 5, 35
Respondents. *See* Avoiders; Compliers; Parents
Robey, John, 57
Rossell, Christine, 8–9, 35

Safety, school. *See* School safety
St. John, Nancy, 71
Sample groups: development of survey instruments for, 33; information sought from, 33; methods of selecting, 31–32; procedures for conducting interviews with, 33–34; similarity of, to population, 32–33. *See also* Avoiders; Compliers; Parents
School characteristics, and avoidance: condition of school neighborhood, 62–63; percent black enrollment, 57–59; percent of black in school neighborhood, 60–62; physical condition, 60; previous status, 59–60
School discipline: and avoidance, 66–67; perceptions of, by race, 84–86
School distance: and approval of desegregation policy, 80–81, 82, 83, 92; and avoidance, 55–56
School districts: differences in, in implementing desegregation, 3–4, 53–54; study of, in Florida, 15–20
School funding, effects of desegregation on, 45–46, 49, 71
School location, and avoidance, 60–63
School officials. *See* Administrators; Public officials
School quality: and avoidance, 4–5, 45–49, 63–67; perceptions of, by race, 84–86, 94
School safety: and avoidance, 66–67; for black children, 72
School status, and avoidance, 59–60. *See also* Costs, of school desegregation policies
Segregationists, reaction of, to desegregation plan impacts, 83–84
Sheatsley, Paul B., 38
Smith, Al, 44
SMSAs. *See* Standard Metropolitan Statistical Areas
Social Status: and avoidance, 5, 35–37, 48–49; and class prejudice, 39–41, 48; and efficacy, 44; of nonsouthern migrants, 38; priority of education and, 46
Standard Metropolitan Statistical Areas (SMSAs), Florida's, 17, 18, 19, 20
Stinchcombe, Arthur L., 6, 8, 57
Student transportation. *See* Busing
Support, parental: attitudinal factor and, 73, 83–84, 85–86, 91–92, 94; desegregation plan impacts, ef-

fect on, 81–84; of desegregation in principle, 73–75; determinants of, 91–96; effects of busing policies on, 79–80; effects of school distance on, 79–81, 92; effect of sense of political efficacy on, 88–89; 92–93; and percent black enrollment in schools, 77–79, 84–86; and perception of school instruction quality, 63–67, 71–72, 84–86; school officials' influence on, 89–91. *See also* Avoiders; Compliers; Parents
Supreme Court, 76, 101
Surrey County, Virginia, extrasystem avoidance in, 4

Teachers, effects of extrasystem avoidance on, 5, 48
Trust, and avoidance, 44–45
Tumin, Melvin M., 35, 39

U.S. Census figures, 61
U.S. Commission on Civil Rights, national survey of, 54
U.S. Department of Health, Education and Welfare, 16
U.S. Department of Justice, 5, 16
U.S. v. *Board of School Commissioners, Indianapolis, Indiana,* 57

"White flight": effect of, on quality of public education, 4–5, 48–49; forms of, 1–2; and percent black enrollment, 57–59; as release of racial tension, 49; research on, 5–9
Wilkerson County, Mississippi, extrasystem avoidance in, 4
Wilmington, Delaware, case, 57

About the Authors

Everett F. Cataldo was educated at Holy Cross College and Ohio State University. At the time of the study reported in this book he was Director of the Institute of Behavioral Research at Florida Atlantic University. He is currently professor and chairman of the Department of Political Science at Cleveland State University.

Micheal W. Giles is associate professor of political science at Florida Atlantic University. He received his bachelor's degree from North Texas State University and earned his doctorate at the University of Kentucky. He has published numerous articles on school desegregation and judicial processes in leading social science journals.

Douglas S. Gatlin is professor and chairman of the Department of Political Science at Florida Atlantic University. A native Floridian, he is a graduate of the University of Florida and earned his doctorate at the University of North Carolina at Chapel Hill. His scholarly interests include American politics and political theory as well as public policy, and he has published books or articles in each of these areas.